THE
TRADE
UNION
PINT

First published in 2012 by
Liberties Press
7 Rathfarnham Road | Terenure | Dublin 6W
Tel: +353 (1) 405 5703
www.libertiespress.com | info@libertiespress.com

Trade enquiries to Gill & Macmillan Distribution
Hume Avenue | Park West | Dublin 12
T: +353 (1) 500 9534 | F: +353 (1) 500 9595 | E: sales@gillmacmillan.ie

Distributed in the UK by
Turnaround Publisher Services
Unit 3 | Olympia Trading Estate | Coburg Road | London N22 6TZ
T: +44 (0) 20 8829 3000 | E: orders@turnaround-uk.com

Distributed in the United States by
Dufour Editions | PO Box 7 | Chester Springs | Pennsylvania | 19425

Copyright © Martin Duffy, 2012
The author has asserted his moral rights.

Paperback ISBN: 978-1-907593-46-8
Hardback ISBN: 978-1-907593-57-4
2 4 6 8 10 9 7 5 3 1
A CIP record for this title is available from the British Library.

Cover design by Sin É Design
Internal design by Liberties Press
Printed by Nørhaven, Denmark

THE TRADE UNION PINT

THE UNLIKELY UNION OF GUINNESS AND THE LARKINS

MARTIN DUFFY

Contents

Acknowledgements

There are people without whose help this book could never have happened. Eibhlin Roche and Deirdre MacParland of the Guinness Archive have been a constant support to me. Ed Penrose's team at the Irish Labour History Society were always seeking to find any material that might be of help to me, as was Carol Murphy of the SIPTU College.

My sister Ethel and her husband Derek Carruthers gave me the vital gift of time to do the research and spend my many hours poring over thousands of documents, exploring articles and books, while trying to tell this story.

My special thanks goes to Jack Harte whom I met several times and also phoned regularly with my questions as I sought to fit the pieces of the puzzle together. I am honoured to have met a true legend – a giant of a man among the many giants in this story. I hope I have served him, his comrades and the brilliant Sir Charles Harvey well in this book. I hope I have not left too many forgotten heroes. This book covers the years up to 1969 and Jack Harte, in helping me in the research and writing, was at pains to point out that there were many trade unionists before and since who have made important contributions. He wrote: 'In our journey to winning negotiation rights we were accompanied by many men and women who took the larger view by showing an interest in their surroundings and the personalities of others. This large group of chief shop stewards, shop stewards and branch committee members played an invaluable role in the growth and development of Number Nine Guinness Branch, the Workers' Union of Ireland.'

Martin Duffy

Foreword

Martin Duffy's study of the unionisation of general staff in the Guinness Brewery is compelling. His story is told, in part, through three central personalities. Charles Harvey, a retired British imperial militarist, was an apparently unsuited managerial appointment in a Brewery facing rapid technological, production and market changes. In addition, he was confronted by the organisation of the non-craft general operatives into the Workers' Union of Ireland (WUI), more than ably led by Jack Carruthers and, later, Jack Harte. The struggle to establish the WUI was difficult but – no more than for Officer Commanding Harvey – Carruthers and Harte drew much tactical inspiration from their respective service in the Irish and British Armies. All three understood leadership, command and strategy. They knew the art of retreat as well as advance. They knew that individual battles were not the war but that certain positions had to be defended to the last. The principle of trade union organisation was their first battleground and one that could not be abandoned at any cost. The WUI's chosen terrain was not an obviously fertile one.

Brewery workers are not found in the vanguard of Labour. Indeed, the trade produced few dedicated trade unions. In Ireland, the only organisations found outside Dublin were in Cork and, surprisingly, Castlebellingham, County Louth. They were short-lived or absorbed by British-based general workers' unions before 1914 or the Irish Transport & General Workers' Union (ITGWU) after 1917. Coopers' Societies, conversely, claimed direct lineage from the Coopers' Guilds. The Dublin Regular Coopers – which operated in Guinness – from 1666, Cork

9

Coopers, 1700, and Belfast Coopers, 1812. Dundalk, Kilkenny, Limerick, Londonderry, Tipperary, and Waterford Societies operated from 1850 at least. By 1895, most had joined the British-based Mutual Association of Journeymen Coopers. With the exception of the Dublin Society – which operated independently until the trade was obliterated by the introduction of metal kegs in the 1960s – they re-established separate existences until the Trade Union Act, 1941, forced their merger with ITGWU. By then, most non-craft brewery workers were ITGWU members.

The exception was Guinness, famous for its 'from cradle to grave' paternalism towards its employees and their families. A St James's Gate Brewery Labourers' Trade Union (SJGBLTU) was established in 1891, while a Dublin Brewery Labourers' Trade Union operated in parallel. The SJGBLTU was a 'company union' and management suppressed it when little upward pressure emanated from a supine workforce. When James Larkin and the ITGWU arrived in 1909, workers in brewers Watkins, Jameson, Pim & Co and Darcy's quickly joined. By 1911, Larkin succeeded in winning a three shillings rise for Guinness 'contractors' men' but the big prize of directly-employed staff remained elusive. It was believed that Guinness general workers remained unorganised until the efforts described so excitingly in Duffy's study, but the ITGWU had some earlier success.

At a mass meeting in Beresford Place on 23 July 1911, Larkin made one of his numerous appeals to 'Guinness's men': 'Is it not time you took your place by your class and organised yourselves?' He noted that Guinness 'does not object to your organising', a supposition based on company dealings with coopers and other crafts. Guinness became alarmed and, in September, hired the Confidential Enquiry Agency of Michael Sheehan, 'late Sergeant, Detective Department, Dublin Castle'. Dealing with a trade union was one thing, being confronted by 'Larkinism' quite another. In addition, as Duffy shows, the Brewery's internal caste system, management's dependence on the Foremen, and the owners' benevolent paternalism, all mitigated against general staffs' unionisation.

But, in 1913 the ITGWU made leeway. The Irish Worker invited 'all Guinness's employees except tradesmen' to attend a meeting at 74 Thomas Street on 26 January: 'It is important that every man in Guinness's employ should attend. Be slaves no longer!' By June, it appeared that about 500 Guinness staff were ITGWU members. Some boatmen were dismissed during the Lockout but the Brewery was largely unaffected by that year's industrial turbulence. ITGWU organisation was maintained until at least June 1920 when John Hill, 'late employee of Messrs Guinness' was dismissed for union activities, 'having acted as Secretary, Brewery Section without remuneration'. After that, organisation among general operatives ceased. By 1947 – Duffy's starting point – even the folk memory of ITGWU activity appeared lost.

It was thus a completely fresh canvass upon which Duffy's leading characters sought to prime their work. Its completed appearance they could never have imagined. Duffy's account has drama, wonderfully detailed characterisation and a pace that gives the work an almost literary feel. But this was no fiction. It was a real life and the unlikely dynamic between Harvey and the men led by Carruthers and Harte transformed the Brewery, enabling it to modernise, reduce costs, improve competitiveness, and suitably reward its staff. As the story concludes, Carruthers ceased to be WUI Branch Secretary. New problems emerged and, to the present, Guinness has continued to automate, outsource and sub-contract, reducing staff and diminishing the Branch's significance within union and broader movement.

WUI No 9 Branch was a flagship. Its value as training ground for Shop Stewards and activists was indicated by the number of Branch Representatives elected to WUI General Executive Committee, the range of Branch motions proposed at Annual Conference, and the eloquence and confidence of those moving them. Carruthers and Harte abhorred member apathy and sectionalism. Reflecting their military experiences, they knew men were best led when well informed, disciplined and committed. They achieved these objectives. Duffy notes that many Guinness members rose to high union positions – notably Paddy Cardiff, who became WUI General Secretary and ICTU President, and Tom Garry, WUI General President and SIPTU General Secretary. They all readily acknowledged their debt to Carruthers, Harte and other Guinness personalities. They had been well-served by James Larkin Junior and Christy Ferguson, central figures in Duffy's early chapters. Larkin's broad and inclusive view of the union branch being central to workers' lives perhaps came closest to achievement in Guinness. Larkin's vision remained central to Carruthers and his confreres.

Reflecting the strong Branch commitment to education and training, John Graham became a Tutor in the ICTU/WUI and SIPTU College. I worked with John and learned of his respect for the trade union grounding he received in the Brewery. Competition for positions as Shop Stewards was intense and attendance at general meetings high. Men were simultaneously proud of their employment and their Union. Often, strong, single-employment union branches suffer from introspective, sectional attitudes. Certainly, much of Guinness members' time was consumed by internal concerns, dealing with the emerging practices of work study and productivity. But Guinness members were among the first to demand opposition to Apartheid; broader national wage agreements that developed into National Understandings and, much later, Social Partnership; and meaningful industrial democracy, including sub-board structures. This latter demand was never meaningfully achieved either within the Brewery or wider workforce. Finally, as a full expression of their broad social concern, Guinness members created a social employment fund, supported by weekly contributions, that developed into Workers' Unity Trust and SIPTU's Irish Trade Union Trust. This provided financial support for co-operative enterprise and social solidarity advice and information.

Duffy's study is a unique view inside an enterprise, examining its industrial and social dynamic. It is well-informed by documented evidence, secondary and oral sources and striking photographs. It is particularly enriched by his access to

Carruthers' autobiographical memoir and Harte's ready memory. It is highly recommended as an important study of Irish industrial relations in the 1950s/1960s, suggesting similar studies for other important employments. Above all, it is thoroughly enjoyable, totally accessible and one of which all those associated with its detail will be proud.

Finally, Guinness was full of characters. Duffy grants us a flavour of their intelligence, their informed demands and their challenge to decisions in which they felt excluded or insufficiently involved. Guinness was seen as a 'good job' but work could be tough and physically demanding. For Carruthers, being Branch Secretary was demandingly all-consuming. Satisfaction came from a personal sense of achievement rather than expressions of membership gratitude. Duffy's study is thus a tribute to Jack Carruthers' commitment, sagacious and foresighted leadership, and unquestioned service to fundamental trade union principle. It is a truly fitting tribute.

Francis Devine,
Musicians' Union of Ireland

An Unlikely Marriage

How do you improve on perfection? The Guinness family were the finest of people – drawn as much to religion as commerce – and they were considered the best employers in Ireland, if not in the world. They cared for their workers' welfare in every way, not only paying them the best rates but also nurturing them both practically and culturally. So why would the workers ever need something as troublesome and cantankerous as a trade union?

This is the story of two families and their allies. They were the most unlikely of partners: model employers the Guinness family, renowned for their standard of care for their staff, and the sons and leaders of a trade union established by 'Big Jim' Larkin, who once declared he was on a 'divine mission of discontent' and whose vision for Irish workers had brought the first open conflict between employer and employee in Ireland. Both families were visionary – one brought trade unionism to Ireland, the other led the way in care for Irish workers.

This test of the Labour movement was not a matter of raising the oppressed up from beneath the control of exploiting employers; it was in proving the value of a trade union even to workers in the employ of a company that was outstanding in its care and foresight. It was often thought that there would never be a trade union in the Guinness Brewery for the simple reason the workers wanted for nothing. That the union chosen by the workers, and accepted by Guinness, was the most radical one in Ireland in its time, is a lesson in the very nature of industrial relations. And grounds for pride on both sides.

The Guinness Brewery was a workers' Utopia. But it was also a Dystopia. No matter how well a second-class citizen is treated, he remains a second-class citizen. The Guinness company would never deliberately oppress its workers. They simply did not realise that their paternalistic approach belittled the 'non-tradesmen' general workers they employed. The awakening – on both sides – is the core of this book.

One

A Changed World

This story begins as the world was picking itself up from the ashes and ruination of the Second World War. When that war ended, three key figures in this book brought to a close three very different war experiences and made their way to the Guinness brewery. Two – Jack Harte and Jack Carruthers – were working-class Dubliners, the third – Sir Charles Harvey – was a man of very worthy British stock. The Dubliners entered the Brewery at the lowest 'non-skilled labourer' level in the Brewery – the Tariff men. The Englishman entered at the highest level of management – a member of the Board of Directors. If the Guinness hierarchy had continued unchanged in the following years, these men at the highest and lowest levels would never have met. In fact, in the years that followed the three became friends.

The new post-war recruit on the management side of the Brewery was Major-General Sir Charles Offley Harvey CB, CVO, CBE, MC. The 'MC' was the Military Cross – awarded in recognition of 'an act or acts of exemplary gallantry during active operations against the enemy'. Harvey was a typical choice for Guinness upper management: just the right mix of religious, military and royal connections. Sir Charles was born in 1888, one of ten children of Vicar F. Clyde Harvey of Sussex. To be the son of a vicar was a plus for anyone in Guinness management; there were church ministers in the Guinness family. He entered the Royal Military College at Sandhurst where he completed training in 1908 and in

1909 he joined the Central India Horse, a cavalry regiment of the British Indian Army.

Harvey spent his military career in India and rose through the officer ranks. He served in the First World War in the Egyptian Expeditionary Force and some years later he acted as assistant military secretary to the Prince of Wales – the man who later would become King Edward the Eighth and then abdicate to marry American divorcee Wallis Simpson – when the prince toured India. Harvey commanded the Indian contingent that attended the coronation of Edward's successor, King George the Sixth, in 1937.

In the Second World War Harvey commanded the Wana Brigade from 1939 to 1940 and then the Eighth Indian Division until 1942. He then became Military Adviser-in-Chief to the Indian State Forces. This man was a model soldier of colonialism, the British Empire and royal rule. He had also, significantly, witnessed the changes from colonialism to independence in India.

In keeping with a life steeped in the military world, Harvey married Lily Millicent Pritchard, daughter of Major-General H. L. Pritchard – a man who had fought in the Siege of Khartoum in 1896. The couple had three children: sons Peter and Charles and daughter Marjorie.

Upon his retirement from military service in 1946, after almost forty years in uniform, Harvey returned to England and was knighted. In the same year he was invited by Lord Iveagh to join the Board of Directors of Guinness. He was appointed as an Assistant Managing Director with particular responsibility for personnel in the Dublin brewery. His position in Guinness was as much a reward as a task: at the level of the Board such men were presented with a workload that was far from strenuous. It was often treated as an honorary job – a reward given to friends of royalty or friends of the Guinness family. Effectively it was a chance for Harvey to enjoy a lucrative niche in the Brewery hierarchy with minimal workload. After all, the word that came up to the Board through lower management and the foremen was that the general workers in the Brewery were well cared-for and content.

Sir Charles was aged fifty-eight, with a distinguished military career behind him, when he arrived in Dublin to live at 98 James's Street – a house provided by the Brewery and facing the gates the men he was responsible for filed through every day and night. His new home was an elegant four-storey house with servant life in the basement providing comfort for their masters above. Harvey was free to sit back and enjoy life as part of the Guinness elite. Life was so comfortable for upper management in the Brewery that they could come into their offices at ten in the morning, pull on their slippers and sit by their fires to read the newspapers until four in the afternoon, interrupted only by a pleasant, long lunch in their own exclusive brewery restaurant. Sir Charles could enjoy his later years in comfort, tucked away in the ivory castle of Guinness senior management's offices. Fortunately, he did not do so.

Harvey was a tall man, elegant and composed, who enjoyed smoking his pipe and drinking a bottle or two of his employer's brew. He loved all sports and encouraged sporting activities among the brewery workers. He would take brisk walks around his new Dublin neighbourhood with his red setter dogs, and maintained his upright military demeanour. He also had a sense of humour: one lunchtime in the Brewery he recommended to a guest that he have a drink of the – higher alcohol content – Guinness Foreign Extra Stout. Harvey, however, only took the normal Extra Stout explaining that 'Foreign always puts me to sleep in the afternoon.' Another director present said 'But you always go to sleep in the afternoon anyway.' Harvey replied, 'Yes, but if I have a "Foreign" I don't wake up when it's time to go home!'

Harvey had come to the Brewery in changing times: and he had the mettle to eventually rise to the challenges presented to him. Not, however, that he greeted the rising tide of non-tradesmen's demands with open arms: it took time for this military man to come around to listening to those under him. An article in the *Irish Times* years later in Harvey's Guinness career described him as 'a man whose mind has never stuck in one groove: he can accept change, new methods, new ideas . . . Even as a regular soldier he had learned that the days of the Balaclava are long past. Men may be prepared to do and die, but they will certainly demand to know the reason why.'

Jack Harte recalled an incident that says much about Harvey. One day Sir Charles, at home, glanced out the window and saw a road worker he thought he recognised. He stared and studied and finally realised: this was a man who had served under him in India. Harvey rushed out to greet the man and shake his hand. He invited him inside for tea and a chat about old times. Harvey was plainly not only a leader but a man who cared about the men he led. This quality would make a crucial difference when he was faced with the rising tide of discontent among brewery workers; for Sir Charles, understanding was as important as ruling. Crucially, he knew how to listen – perhaps even more importantly he learned who it was he should listen to – and he knew how to change. Lord Iveagh probably didn't realise how lucky he was when he hired this man.

There is a story in Jack Harte's book, *To the Limits of Endurance*, about his World War Two experiences, that says much about the second man destined to be one of the key characters in the unionising of the Guinness brewery and in the Labour movement itself.

In a set of events worthy of being part of a classic war movie, Harte and the other prisoners of war in Stalag XIA had been ordered to salute the German officers but a delegation of the prisoners went to the camp Commander to state they were not obliged to do so. When the Commander dismissed them, the delegation stood their ground to demand an answer – and were locked in solitary confinement for ten days. Jack wrote:

> We realised that we had little choice but to salute the German offi-
> cers, but we hadn't surrendered yet. We organised things so that
> three or four of us would deliberately walk across the path of the
> officers, forcing them to return our salute. This continued all day
> every day, almost wearing them out, until eventually it dawned on
> them what we were up to. They soon made themselves scarce,

doing a speedy about-turn whenever they saw us approach, and the requirement to salute them soon petered out.

Jack Harte was born in Dublin in 1920, one of eleven children. He was a troublesome bundle of energy who wanted to escape unemployment in depressed Ireland and have a taste of the adventure in the British Army already being enjoyed by his brother Tom. When he reached his early teens he stowed away on the ferry to Liverpool. He arrived penniless and went to the Army recruiting office where he lied about his age. Jack joined the Royal Irish/Royal Enniskillen Fusiliers and there followed eight years of military service and adventures that brought him to the brink of death in a German POW camp.

He lived through as much adventure as he sought and more. When he was caught by the Germans in Greece late in the war he reflected: 'I thanked God for my luck, after five long years in combat. I had survived ambushes and engagements in Palestine in 1938, the siege of Malta, being depth-charged in a submarine, raids into enemy-occupied territory, three weeks patrolling the North African and Sicilian coasts on an MTB, and finally, all the fighting on the Greek island Leros.'

Ahead of him was the surviving of life in a POW camp in Germany. The camp held French, Polish and Russian soldiers and Jack, despite his weakened condition, took part in a boxing tournament to rustle up some supplies for his comrades and to raise morale. Wily and indomitable, Jack lived through two years as a prisoner of war while engaging in all kinds of adventures and intrigues to survive and help his fellow prisoners survive.

One thing that Jack Harte, Jack Carruthers and Charles Harvey had in common was that each was 'a man's man'. What Harte perhaps learned in his war days was that when men – no matter what differences between them there might be – teamed up against their 'masters' they could triumph. He suffered starvation, dysentery and hardship as he was moved on from one stalag to another. His book is a marvellous record of the triumph of the human spirit. Given what the future had in store for him, it is a curious coincidence that on his safe return to England his fondest and most vivid memory was of sneaking out of hospital to enjoy, with his brother Gunner Archie Harte, a few pints of Guinness.

For Jack Carruthers, World War Two was 'The Emergency'. He remained in his native Ireland and was one of the many who joined the national force that made itself ready for war while mostly dealing with the practicalities of helping the new-born nation stay safe, fed and heated in such troubled times.

Jack was the son of a Dublin Metropolitan Policeman and grew up in Marino, Dublin. He was an active youth, joining the Boy Scouts and enjoying such activities as camping and boxing. In his teens he developed a passion for motorcycling, and in the army he joined the Irish Cavalry Division which had, in fact, no horses but instead the men were motorcyclists. He became part of an elite trained by motorcycle-racing legend and fellow Dubliner Stanley Woods (known as 'The Irish Dasher') who had joined the army when war broke out.

Being in the Irish Army was a character-forming experience for Jack. He loved the discipline and the need for self-reliance. He was a natural observer of men, and – again something that would shape his later career – he could step back and see social structures. As he wrote: 'One learned to accept responsibility for others and to command, and to appreciate the logic of the organisation and command structure.' He developed a contempt for officers, all of whom came from privileged backgrounds, and he developed strong Socialist leanings. Jack was an avid reader. In this phase of his young manhood he read Karl Marx's *Das Kapital*. He also read the writings of James Connolly. While nations were at war in the rest of the world, Jack was waking up to the war between classes in his own land. He was discovering the work of 'Big Jim' Larkin and the trade union movement. He was waking up to unfinished social business that dated back to the 1913 Dublin Lockout.

The army was a great adventure for Private Jack Carruthers (number 211093). He taught boxing but loved, in particular, the motorcycle rough-riding courses.

He did a course in 'advanced motorcycle riding' and became a dispatch rider in the Second Field Signals. He later did a motorcycling instructor's course and so became an instructor himself. His Army record also notes an Act of Gallantry on his part in November 1944, though no details of the act itself are given. Towards the end of the war he took part in Irish Army motorcyclists' stunt performances in the Military Tattoo.

His wartime experiences were a training ground for the years that lay ahead of him in Guinness. Jack wrote in his family memoir:

> The Army life presented me with a whole new perspective of life as I had up to then experienced it. It provided a comradeship one could never experience in civilian life, as everything was shared and all were subjected to the same disciplines. Very soon one had a pride in one's personal appearances and I enjoyed all the courses on physical fitness and learning new skills with rifles, bayonets, Webleys, not to mention the motorcycle rough riding courses. One also learned to accept responsibility for others and to command, and to appreciate the logic of the organisation and Command structure. Acceptance of the then very strict discipline and understanding of its necessity, particularly in times of stress, when an emotional reaction and not a logical analysis could lead to self-destruction and creating of a greater problem than the one causing the stress in the first place.
>
> Having to look after all your own clothes and equipment, some-times darning one's own socks and repairing one's shirts, sewing on buttons, and when in the 'field', cooking under the most primitive conditions with whatever one could beg, borrow or steal; or literally suffer from malnutrition as war-time Army meals were never ade-quate for fit young men. Even if one had money there was no use going into the villages as there was nothing to buy due to rationing.
>
> There was an aspect of Army life that opened my eyes to the meaning of the socially privileged as even in wartime conditions the officer class lived very well and enjoyed even in the 'field', the serv-ice of home comforts, i.e. good books, Bat Men (servants), cigs, good clothes and sleeping accommodation, not to mention good food.
>
> There was the usual share of egotistical bastards and snobs among the officer class and they were usually the least competent and

weak-kneed, most of whom would have been shot by our own side under actual war conditions.

To understand why this was so one had to bear in mind that many of these 'officers' came from privileged backgrounds, i.e. sons of Army officers, tds, Doctors, Lawyers, the Universities, and the most obnoxious of all, the ignorant sons of publicans and large farmers. Before the War, many of the 'Emergency Officers' were bank managers, civil servants etc. They, as I, were reared in a much more rigid structure (than today) where 'class' was clearly defined and one's 'superiors' (based on age, job, home address) and family connections, were the accepted criteria of one's social standing, not to be challenged without dire consequences. To continue about the 'officer class' of the type I have criticised, (and almost without exception I am excluding the regular Curragh College trained ones, as they were real professional soldiers in every sense of the word) they brought into the Army their civilian type social inhibitions of snobbery, class consciousness and lack of understanding of the ordinary 'Joe Soap' and what was worse they had no inclination or desire to do so. It would have been anathema to their social beliefs. As a consequence of what I observed in these unfair and discriminatory social relationships, I obviously developed a strong desire to do something about establishing and having recognised the dignity of the 'ordinary man', irrespective of his social background or upbringing.

I had soldiered with men much rougher and tougher than I was becoming; human wrecks after only 56 days in the 'glass house' in the Curragh at the hands of our Red Caps (military police).

Jack knew the nature of men and worked to steer them to where he believed they should go. This did not make him an obvious, brash leader. But it did make him an effective and inspiring one. Carruthers, Harte and Harvey shared military experience that formed them. They shared a passage through the war that informed them. All three had been war heroes and had grown through the war years. Their destinies met in a place that had been growing for almost two hundred years.

Brewing beer is a very basic process dating back many thousands of years: a grain such as wheat or barley is malted (germinated and quickly dried) and then roasted. The duration of the roasting decides the ultimate colour of the beer. The next step is to soak, or as it is known 'mash', this substance in a vessel called a 'tun' or 'kieve'. Water is then added to create a sugary liquid called wort. This is boiled and flavoured, most likely with hops (a flower). This liquid is allowed to cool and then yeast is added and fermentation begins – meaning that the yeast, over time, converts the sugars to both carbon dioxide and the ethanol that transforms the liquid into an alcoholic beverage.

Brewing on an industrial scale, as Arthur Guinness started doing in 1759, involves all of those stages writ large. As demand for his porter, later stout, increased, his business expanded to meet demand. His sixty-acre site near the River Liffey, and in the heart of Dublin city, evolved into an industrial principality with its own electricity generation plant; its own railway system (with some eight miles of track); its own fire brigade; tunnel system; medical and social workers, with doctors and pharmacy; post office; printing works and banks. The Guinness brewery that Carruthers, Harte and Harvey began work in was the largest in the world and was producing millions of pints per day of its one product, with the variations of 'porter' 'stout' and 'foreign': the beloved 'pint of plain'. By 1946, when all three men were working in the Brewery, its output for the year was ninety million gallons of the black stuff.

The drink was considered not only delicious but healthy. 'Guinness is Good for You' was a long-lived slogan for the brew that was even recommended by doctors for conditions such as insomnia and nervous troubles, and given to nursing mothers: it would have been good for them, too, as bottles of stout in those days had a yeast sediment at the bottom that would have been rich in Vitamin B. Demand for Guinness, particularly among Dublin men, never flagged despite any ups and downs over the almost two centuries of its existence to the end of the Second World War. Harvey was a Managing Director overseeing a consistently successful brewery with some 3,500 employees. Far away from Sir Charles Harvey's quiet office, down among the 2,800 minions, Carruthers and Harte worked in the labour-intensive steaming world of the Stokers, Spargers, Hop Men and Wort Men who served the coppers, the kieves, the barges and the malt trains.

Edward Cecil Guinness, the first Earl of Iveagh, believed that you couldn't expect to earn money from a man if you did not help him to earn money. With the Guinness success it was particularly so: the working man put his coins on the counter to buy a glass of the brew his fellow working man had worked to produce. No one ever stopped to think that the 'non-tradesmen' in the brewery, who were four-fifths of its workforce, were the real bosses in that they were the financial and physical engines of Guinness's St James's Gate brewery.

The Guinness working structure was a rigid and long-established hierarchy. There were even seven different dining rooms and canteens marking the status of the employees. The levels above the rank (and it really was in effect a military structure) of foreman had no communication with the levels below. Such was the culture of elitism that while a non-trade labourer might eventually rise to the level of foreman – his only possible route away from labouring all his working life – he could never be put in charge of skilled tradesmen. He certainly would never reach management level. There was no bridge between the weekly-paid labourer and the monthly-paid staff.

Finbar Flood, in his excellent autobiography *In Full Flood*, gives a small but very telling anecdote about just how embedded the social structure was when he started in the Brewery as a 'boy messenger' working under 'man messenger' Jim Daly:

> The calling of employees by their surnames was reminiscent of the army and typified the autocratic structures that prevailed in the company. Even men messengers of a 'mature age' were called by their surnames by young women who had just joined the company!
>
> On one occasion, I can remember standing with Jim Daly – Mr Daly, as we addressed him – when a number of young girls passed on their break. One new girl called out 'Hello, Mr Daly' as she passed. He turned to me and said: 'That little girl lives near us. You can see the difference good breeding makes.' The same girl passed a few days later and called out 'Good morning, Daly' to him.

In a very short time, she had learned how the Guinness hierarchy operated.

Managers had their protection and privilege. Craftsmen had their guilds and unions. Craftsmen were fitters, plumbers, coopers etc. The Brewery had one plasterer. Each craft had a guild and each guild had one vote, so the plasterer had a vote just as a guild with 100 members had a vote. The guilds of these crafts were long established and had long ago learned how to get comfortable working conditions for themselves. The majority of the Brewery's employees – the non-tradesmen – depended on the exceptionally benign nature of their employers.

At the top of this world was the polished-wood sedateness in which Sir Charles Harvey lived. At the bottom was the majority of employees: the semi-skilled and non-skilled manual labourers on a five-and-a-half day, forty-four-hour week in shifts that kept the Brewery going around the clock. Work at their level in the Brewery was physically demanding, which was why strong men like boxers and athletes Jack Carruthers and Jack Harte were hired. While the brand and brewery were quintessentially Dublin, Guinness had a declared preference for hiring good strong farmers' sons. These solid and hard-working men who sweated for their wages were the ones who did not have a unified voice.

As 'The Emergency' was drawing to a close it was clear that a flood of man-power was about to be back on 'civvy street'. The Irish government called on all major employers – State and non-State – to hire the men returning from the Irish Army to civilian life. At the end of World War Two the Guinness Brewery decided it would hire equal numbers of men from the British and Irish armies. And so the paths of the two Jacks were destined to cross.

Jack Carruthers got a job in the Cooperage Department as a sawyer, making the staves for the wooden barrels in which the Guinness was delivered to pubs. It was a semi-skilled grade and his job was at a saw machine cutting the strips of American white oak to be curved and bound through the centuries-old art of the cooper to make the barrels for the distribution of the beer. This was a large section, described as being almost as big an operation as the Brewery itself, with

150 coopers and 450 other employees. The section had 320,000 casks in circulation, the lives of the casks tracked by boys who were 'number takers'. The emptied casks were brought back to the Brewery where they were repaired if necessary and where casks were cleaned for re-use. That cleaning process, done in intense steam, was one of the toughest jobs in the Brewery and Carruthers was lucky not to be in that section.

Both Carruthers and Harte were 'tariff men', meaning they were at the lowest level of the Brewery's structure. Jack Harte worked in the kieves – where the mash of ingredients was strained and rinsed with hot water over a false bottom to extract the 'sweet wort' for fermentation. He had a tough job: there were open railway wagons under the kieves that took the spent grain to be sold as cattle feed. Clearing the kieves for the next load was a gruelling job carried out by half-naked men in canvas trousers and wooden clogs. For his first three years, Harte's job was to release the load from the kieves and then shovel it down into the wagons. It was brutally hard work in extreme heat: he and his co-worker would set down a plank on the steaming-hot grain. 'You had to throw down a baker's board to stand on,' Jack recalled, 'otherwise you'd get scalded. The wort was still runny, and once you pulled the caps out of the two holes in the kieve even grabbing on to the chain wouldn't save you so you had to keep well back away from the hole. You had to have a platform to make a footing for yourself and then you started to dig the stuff away. You then stood on the copper plates to shovel the grain down.'

When Harte began working at Guinness Brewery, however, he was considered to be 'on the wrong side' because he had served in the British Army and was treated with suspicion by Irish men he worked with who had Republican leanings. Jack Harte was still weak from his war experiences, and the work was very physically demanding for him at the beginning. The job was done by two men, and the man Harte was teamed with was frustrated by his slowness.

'I don't feel well,' Harte explained.

'Were you in hospital?' the man asked.

'Hitler did it,' Harte replied, joking. His co-worker helped Harte, but when the job was done the man said: 'You're very fortunate I helped you – I'm a fuckin' Republican!'

But the spirit of camaraderie was good among the Guinness men and differences about which side they had been on were forgotten. The work was hard and even dangerous – men died in brewery accidents. But the Guinness flowed freely for the workers, who were given two pints a day as standard and could get up to eight pints more from the foreman for working quicker to get a particular task done. Time was of the essence to keep production moving. Some workers would leave their jobs drunk at the end of their shift and then head straight for the pub!

As Jack Harte recalled, the management on the factory floor had cut out very handsome sinecures for themselves. The foremen would tell the managers what to report to the Board – and this was always giving the impression that the workers were happy and all was well. If any man wanted to go to management with a grievance, the foreman would sit him down, ply him with a few pints, and remind him how lucky he was to be working in the Brewery. The peace was kept: a man would be crazy to risk losing his Guinness job.

This world onto itself had a dark side, the worst surely being the uniformed Brewery Police: men who sometimes hid in the rafters of the building to look down on the employees. These police were in the habit of bursting in the doors of the toilets and accusing the men of smoking even when they were not. It happened to Jack Carruthers a few times in his early years. There was also a man known as the 'jacks clerk' who made sure that the men only went to the toilet the permitted number of times in a shift. He would hand out two sheets of toilet paper and take the workers' pay disc, then record how long the worker stayed in the toilet. For all its benign characteristics, Arthur Guinness Son and Co Ltd did not endear itself to all its workers.

Carruthers gives an angry description of the Guinness structure into which he was hired in his family memoir:

> The Brewery was run on very strict military-type command, each rank being clearly defined and economical death the penalty for

any breach of the accepted norms. The top management were 99% Protestant and/or Free Masons. The next level of Gods (in their own estimation) were the Brewers, Doctors and Department Managers, with their absolute power of economic life or death over every employee. Their power was unquestioned and unchallenged. As a great philosopher said: 'power corrupts, absolute power corrupts absolutely.'

This socially and morally corrupt structure was ably supported from beneath by employing as staff only the products of the universities (Trinity, Eton, Cambridge etc) or some of the sons of well-heeled publicans, farmers etc. who were mentally well suited to maintain the very strict class distinction and who saw nothing morally wrong in screwing and treating the humble labourer as dispensable industrial shit, seldom addressed by name but asked to identify himself by his Brewery Number only. These 'gentlemen' epitomised all that the class struggle stood for and it was their intellectual stupidity in not recognising that ordinary workers understood the meaning of personal dignity that was the Sword of Damocles hanging over their own snobbish heads – the cause of mental illiteracy that prevented them from being able to read the writing on the wall.

They were ably supported from beneath by the non-staff or Labouring Foremen and Chargers who, almost without exception, achieved their position because of religion, usefulness to their superiors and through nepotism of the worst kind.

Since entry to the Brewery at fourteen years of age was on a competitive basis, the boys selected always felt themselves far superior intellectually to the common herd of labouring men, employed for his physical ability to do the very hard work.

This created a distinct 'elite' in the labouring ranks and the 'ex-boy' complex dominated promotion prospects, narrowing the field of selectivity to this 'elite' each in turn ensuring that Foreman status was only achieved within this narrow confine.

The 'lick spittles' and 'arse lickers' who were not 'ex-boys', who acted as the Foreman's extra eyes and ears, could aspire to getting an extra Grade or being made Chargers – the lowest administration rank in the Brewery.

This system ensured that the basic labourer, through fear of economic strangulation, thought only of their own personal survival.

Guinness supplied a hugely popular product so there was no need to cut corners or count the pennies. The employees who were non-skilled had no say in the running of the company but they were also generously cared for. The Guinness brewery was a very comfortable world onto itself: the waft of its brewing work drifting out around the surrounding area in Dublin, where one in thirty citizens were dependent on it, and the blanket of its care securely tucking in its loyal employees. No one could want for anything more.

Right?

Guinness was an industrial iceberg: all that was visible was the Board, the honourable family ethos and the beloved brand. Under the surface was the massive force of manual labourers driving the engine, staying silent and being nourished by their benevolent masters. Guinness needed to wake up. The lives of Sir Charles and the two Jacks intersected at the crossroads formed by the meeting of the company and the Workers' Union of Ireland. Leading that union was a man who oversaw the extraordinary shift of Guinness to the point where they not only accepted the unionising of their general workers, but even made trade union membership a condition of employment. This man, who led the process of flattening the Guinness pyramid, was James Larkin Jr. He was the eldest son of the man who had transformed the lives of Ireland's working class: the charismatic, fearless, flawed, divisive and controversial 'Big Jim' Larkin – a man whose approach to worker/employer relationships was a far cry from any genteel Guinness view of keeping the workers happy while ignoring them. A man who showed the cowered Dublin worker how to rise up.

Two

Larkin's Rabble

The slow growth of trade unionism in Ireland in the nineteenth century was an expansion of self-interest groups. The skilled and craft workers – printers, bakers, plumbers, carpenters and so on – who made up a third of the workforce gathered under the banners of their trades with specific aims: to limit the number of apprentices brought in, to monitor that their job was not done by non-skilled workers and to protect their pay and working conditions.

When these unions gathered in Dublin in 1894 for the first Irish Trade Union Congress their hospitality fund was sponsored by employers including William Martin Murphy who, as main shareholder of the Dublin United Tramway Company, also saw to it that the union delegates received free passes for the trams. The event was very polite and self-congratulatory. The President of the first congress, a carpenter named Thomas O'Connell, cautioned against using the right to strike or seeking to enforce an eight-hour day. This way of organising labour became known as 'old unionism', with its Associations, Guilds and Societies.

Far from that cosy gathering in Dublin a 'new unionism' was emerging in England where trade unionism was developing stronger links with the Labour movement and socialist beliefs: a development the Irish employers did not want to see repeated in their backyard. But even for the working class elite of craftsmen, interest in trade unions was sluggish and there were proportionally far fewer Trade Union Congress members in Ireland than in Scotland or England. The most contentious matter on the agenda for the unions was not social injustice but conflict between those unions who were solely Irish and those who were amalgamated to British unions – the latter being mainly in the north of Ireland.

One man, born in Edinburgh of Irish parents, had moved to Dublin in 1896 and tried to stir up social change as secretary of the Dublin Socialist Society which later evolved into the Irish Socialist Republican Party: this was James Connolly. Feeling that he was not making progress, he moved to America in 1903 to continue his socialist agitation. The ITUC rolled gently along for over a decade, its main concern always the protection of the working conditions and elitism of their members. Employers and tradesmen were happy while the unskilled general workers remained defenceless, poor and downtrodden.

All this changed when 'Big Jim' Larkin came to Ireland.

Larkin was born in Liverpool in 1876 to Irish emigrant parents. His working life started when he was nine years old. As a teenage sailor he travelled to South America, and back in Liverpool he worked as a docker and rose to the position of foreman. He lost that job in 1905, then a young married man with a one-year-old son named James Jr, when he joined a strike with the men working under him. This extraordinary act of courage led to his being hired by James Sexton, general secretary of the National Union of Dock Labourers and fellow Liverpudlian of Irish parents, as an organiser.

Larkin was sent first to Scotland and, in 1907, to Belfast to recruit members for the Union where he had great success. Membership among carters and porters in Belfast boomed and there was soon strike action and public unrest. So enigmatic was the man that there was a myth born that he even brought the Royal Irish Constabulary out on strike by pointing out to them that they were having to work many unpaid extra hours trying to keep the protesting dockers under control! He had a powerful impact on the labour situation in the port city of Belfast causing huge disruptions in the form of a labour lockout at the docks and a march of an estimated 100,000 Catholics and Protestants through the streets of the city in protest at the lockout. On the Twelfth of July, he marched arm in arm with the head of the Orange Lodge leading 11,000 Catholic and Protestant strikers. As Larkin launched into blazing attacks on employers, Belfast was suddenly thrown into a chaos of riots. Larkin knew how to inflame passions, and his oratory was later described by American Communist scholar Bertram Wolfe, in his book *Strange Communists I Have Known* thus:

> 'When Larkin spoke, his blue eyes flashed and sparked. He roared and thundered. Sometimes an unruly forelock came down on his forehead as he moved his head in vigorous emphasis. Impulsive, fiery, passionate, swift at repartee, highly personal, provocative, and hot-tempered in attack, strong and picturesque of speech, Larkin's language was rich in the turns of Irish poetic imagery sprinkled with neologisms of his own devising.'

No wonder he struck fire in the hearts of the workers and fear in the hearts of the employers. Larkin's rousing of the dock workers in Belfast proved to be a trial run for events to come in Dublin and was a noble failure. After all the riots, speeches, lockouts, scab labour and failed interventions the dust settled back on the old ways of doing things. Larkin, though considered a hero for leading the workers and raising their morale and consciousness, had done so at the cost of great hardship and even their jobs. Many who had joined his union had been kicked out of work.

NUDL then sent Larkin to Dublin in 1908 to continue his work of recruiting new members. What he saw in Dublin appalled him and would transform the lives of worker and employer there alike. Swearing to get justice against the ruthless employers, he said, with his typical gift for oration: 'Christ will not be crucified any longer in Dublin by these men.'

Dublin was considered to have the worst slums in Europe. It had the highest infant mortality rate and lowest life expectancy of any city in the United Kingdom. Homes that had been the town houses of the gentry were sold off over the decades to landlords who let them fall into decay while renting them out as slum dwellings for families of up to fifteen living in a room. One of Larkin's early projects was to document this situation to pressure for housing improvements. An investigation into the tenements showed that two thirds were unfit for human habitation. Dublin in the early twentieth century had a population of 300,000. Of these, a third were destitute and living in tenement slums – in many cases with up to a hundred people in a house served by one toilet and one water tap in the shared courtyard. These were the homes of the unskilled 'general workers' who lived from hand to mouth without a voice and – if they had a job at all – without job security. Food prices had been rising since the start of the century with no pay increases to balance this. Poverty and prostitution were endemic.

Larkin realised that his first task was to inspire and uplift these people who had known powerlessness for so many generations that they believed in no other possible fate. He was the right man for the challenge. He was a brilliant orator and this six-foot-four, blue-eyed man with his booming voice instilled hope in the Irish working class. One of his most famous quotes was 'The great only appear great because you are on your knees. Rise up!'

'Big Jim' Larkin's impact on trade union membership was immediate and dramatic. Within a year he had recruited 2,700 dock workers in Dublin to the National Union of Dock Labourers and established a branch of the Irish Labour Party in Dublin. But he also launched three strikes and the NUDL, alarmed by his continual radical approach and the cost to the union of his actions, fired him. An ongoing theme of Larkin's life was also an element in this: he'd had a personality clash with his boss, James Sexton, and the two could no longer work together. Larkin had an unfortunate knack of fighting personalities rather than causes and thereby accumulating enemies. After being fired from the NUDL, he was later charged with misappropriating union funds (to help striking dock workers in Cork) and sentenced to a year in prison. This was commuted to three months.

Undaunted by the break from the NUDL, Larkin had now seen the bigger picture of the needs of the unskilled labour force in Ireland: three-quarters of Irish workers were agricultural, domestic or general labourers with no united voice and thus living at the mercy of their employers. Larkin decided to form the Irish Transport and General Workers' Union to raise these people up out of poverty and give them rights and dignity in their working lives. James Connolly soon returned from the USA to become a full-time official of the ITGWU, based in Belfast. Meanwhile Larkin's sister, Delia, set up the Irish Women Workers' Union. A left-wing Dublin trade unionist, the tailor William O'Brien, also joined forces with Larkin. There was hope of change – if not revolution.

With Larkin in town, the cosy 'old unionism' was shaken to its roots at the annual Irish Trade Union Congress. He was elected to its parliamentary committee and the ITGWU was accepted into the Congress. By 1911, the ITGWU paid Congress affiliation fees for 5,000 members, making it the largest delegation. In that year Larkin also launched the radical publication *The Irish Worker* – which he largely wrote. Within months its circulation quadrupled to 100,000.

James Plunkett, the devoted 'Larkinite' and eventual trade union official working for Larkin, quoted this piece as a typical example of Larkin's writing:

> At present you spend your lives in sordid labour, your abode in filthy slums; your children hunger and your masters say your slavery must endure forever. If you would come out of bondage you yourself must forge the weapons and fight the grim battle.

Plunkett wrote the classic novel about this era: *Strumpet City*. It is the bittersweet epic tale of the awakening of the Dublin working class. Jim Larkin was indeed inspiring the workers to 'rise up': he said he wanted them not only to have bread on the table but a vase of flowers, too.

Inevitably, in this campaign, Larkin found an archenemy: William Martin Murphy who, years before, had been so generous in his support of the ITUC that he sponsored their event and gave the delegates free tram passes but who now saw the need for employers to keep the workers on their knees. Mogul and major shareholder of the Dublin United Tramway Company, as well as owner of the newspaper the *Irish Independent* and its Sunday and evening versions, Murphy was an early target of Larkin's vitriol and warned other employers to fight off what his publications referred to as 'Larkin's rabble of carters and dockers'. For his part, Larkin declared to Murphy through *The Irish Worker* that: 'We will drive you to defeat, or we will break your heart.'

As membership of the ITGWU grew, Larkin could afford to move its headquarters from a two-room office to the former Northumberland Hotel at 18 Beresford Place. The building was renamed Liberty Hall and was used not only as the Union's base but as a social centre for workers. With the growth of the Union came the growth of industrial unrest. It would seem also that the mounting work pressure on Larkin made him a more volatile character subject to bouts of elation and depression. He was a difficult man to work with and James Connolly once wrote to William O'Brien: 'I don't think I can stand Larkin as boss much longer. He is singularly unbearable. He is consumed with jealousy and hatred of anyone who will not cringe to him and beslaver him all over.'

One of Larkin's main targets was to unionise the non-trade workers in the Guinness brewery. For all the unrest and rebellion that Larkin was creating among the Dublin working class, however, his call to battle never reached inside St James's Gate. It was too safe in there for the workers to join in any industrial agitation.

In an irony that hopefully was not lost on the greedy and fearful Dublin employers, four hundred of them gathered together under the banner of their newly-formed Employers' Federation for precisely the goal of preventing the general workers from joining under a banner of their own. Murphy started firing workers in his various companies, including the Irish Independent and Dublin Tramways, who were members of the ITGWU, and replacing them with 'scab' labour.

The fight was on. Larkin gave a speech after which he was arrested for incitement, but he was released in the face of the huge public outcry. He announced another mass meeting on Dublin's main street – then named Sackville Street – but the Magistrate banned it. Larkin swore he would make the speech regardless and the street was packed with many thousands waiting for him on the day.

The crowd was cordoned by hundreds of police officers, many of them brought in as reserves from outside the city. Larkin, in disguise as an old man accompanied by his niece, managed to get to the balcony of The Imperial Hotel – which was owned by Murphy – and began addressing the crowd. He was quickly arrested.

Then one of the ugliest scenes in the city's history ensued as the Dublin Metropolitan Police baton-charged the crowd causing hundreds of injuries – there had been two deaths in baton-charge days previously – and destroying the public's faith in their own police force. Reports on the bloody scenes spread across the world. Riots continued into the following day, with police even going into the tenements to attack the people in their homes and destroy their few belongings. Murphy, quoted in his *Irish Independent*, said: 'I have broken the malign influence of Mr Larkin and set him on the run.'

One of the men who had been killed in the first riot, James Nolan, was buried on 3 September 1913. On that same day, William Murphy – obviously not a man bothered by sentiment or sympathy – convened a meeting of the Employers' Federation at which he presented what became known as 'the document'. This obliged their employees to sign a declaration that they would not join the ITGWU or that if already a member of the union they would leave it immediately. Larkin's followers were loyal to him and would not sign the declaration demanded by the Employers' Federation. Furthermore, many of the craft unions supported the ITGWU members. The battle lines were drawn. The employers' response was to show their power over the workers by shutting the gates of their factories and businesses: the Dublin Lockout had begun.

The Lockout took a terrible toll on the poor of the city. Dublin's working class, already suffering extremes of poverty, now faced starvation. Larkin, released from prison, set about the desperate two-prong struggle for financial and militant support. Soup kitchens were run from Liberty Hall. Larkin organised a food ship from England and the TUC there donated five thousand pounds to the Dublin workers with the promise of weekly support to follow. Larkin organised rallies throughout Britain to gather support for sympathetic strikes or for blocking 'tainted goods' – product for any employer using 'scab' labour. One such Dublin employer was the Guinness brewery. This action was not forthcoming from the English unions, however, and Larkin became ever more bitter and critical, engaging in yet more personal battles with English trade union chiefs.

The Lock-out lasted for seven months before dying out with neither side giving way. Yet it was a moral victory for the workers because the employers quietly withdrew their demand that employees not become members of the ITGWU – it was a psychological victory not unlike the one Harte and his comrades had over the Nazi soldiers in the POW camp who had been demanding that they be saluted. Most importantly, for all the misery of the Lockout it showed the Dublin working class that they could indeed, no matter how high the price and how limited the gain, rise up. This trial by fire had been the true birth of the labour movement in Ireland. A change had occurred in the mind-set of the working class. By the end of the ordeal Larkin was exhausted but undefeated. He left Ireland and would spend the next ten years in the USA, first raising funds but then getting embroiled in the politics of his new homeland. He became a vocal supporter of the Soviet Union and was such a radical that he was even expelled from the Socialist Party of America. He ended up in Sing Sing prison in 1920 serving a sentence of up to ten years for 'criminal anarchy'.

Meanwhile, the Guinness brewery and brand escaped notice, gliding through with flying colours, its porter still the darling of the working man. Larkin's two main targets for unionising labour had been the Dublin United Tramway Company and the city's biggest employer: the Guinness Brewery. While William Martin Murphy gained the nickname 'William Murder Murphy' in the course of the Lockout, the Guinness family, and their brew, remained as beloved as ever through those terrible months and beyond.

By the time of the Lockout, 400 of Guinness's 3,500-strong labour force had joined the ITGWU. Murphy met representatives of the Guinness board, urging them to join the federation but the company declined. Guinness employees were not forced to sign the anti-ITGWU declaration form concocted by the Federation, so the union members were not confronted and the Brewery maintained a low profile throughout the drama. The company did, however, secretly donate £5,000 to the Federation in the course of the Lockout – a fact it later tried to conceal. It may have been that Guinness did not want to risk becoming the target of Larkin's 'tainted goods' strike strategy: to identify the pint of plain as made by an anti-union employer would have been to lower it from the lips of the working class men who were its entire market.

But Guinness's reputation as an employer and as a benefactor for the working class was unassailable. And rightly so. Given the oppression suffered by almost all other general workers in Dublin, life for the non-tradesmen – for all Guinness employees – was a life of privilege. It was an oasis in Strumpet City. Guinness employees already enjoyed the kind of working lives Larkin would have aimed to achieve, through the ITGWU, for all workers.

Labourers in the Guinness brewery were paid up to 20 percent more than other workers in Ireland. They also received a daily supply of pints of their brew – with extra pints given as incentives for tasks. The Brewery provided subsidised meals for its employees and encouraged them to further education. At a time when most people worked for low pay and with no security or pension, Guinness voluntarily provided a pension which continued for the employee's widow after the employee's death. While the State provided a pension of five shillings a week from the age of seventy, Guinness gave its labourers a pension of seventeen shillings a week from the age of sixty. Guinness had a full-time medical staff providing 24-hour care for the employees and their families, including making house calls. Guinness even provided housing for their employees having, at their own initiative through their own Chief Medical Officer John Lumsden (a visionary man of saint-like compassion; there should be a monument to him in Dublin), done a thorough investigation of the housing conditions of their employees. They did all this of their own free will. No wonder it was with pride that a woman could say she was 'married to a Guinness man'.

The philosophy of the company, shaped by the strong Christian commitments of the Guinness family, made them model employers and pillars of Irish society. In 1877 when St Stephen's Green was changed from a private park for local residents to a public park, the then head of the Guinness family paid for the work needed to redesign it. All down the generations, members of the Guinness family were drawn as much to religious and social work as they were to industry. They set up the Iveagh Trust for the benefit of the poor of Dublin and London. John Lumsden devoted himself, on behalf of the company, to improving the health and living conditions of Dublin's poor. When Rupert Guinness (who had been given five million pounds by his father when he reached the age of twenty-one) married Lady Gwendolyn Owen in London in October 1903, his father gave him a gift of a house in St James's Square in London: Rupert and his new wife moved instead for a time into a tenement house in the Shoreditch area. Rupert devoted much of his time and wealth to slum clearance. This was a family business run by the most honourable of families: unlike William 'Murder' Murphy, they were the friends of the Dublin working class.

That said, during the Lockout Guinness brought 'scab' labour from England and, as Larkin put it, 'the wilds of Tipperary' to unload barley from the docks and bring it to the Brewery. In the course of this, Guinness also fired six men who would not handle an import of barley they considered 'tainted goods'. The company refused, despite direct written pleas from Jim Larkin and James Connolly, to reinstate these men. To lose a Guinness job was a particularly grievous blow to any family.

The Dublin Lockout ended in early 1914 and within months Dublin, Ireland and the world would be rocked by the next quake in a relentless flow of turmoil. When the First World War broke out many Irish volunteered with over 200,000 Irishmen in combat. James Connolly described it as 'economic conscription' as there was no employment to be had in Ireland and a soldier's wage was double that of the average labourer's. Typical of its honourable ethos, Guinness said it would continue to pay a half-wage to an employee who joined the army and guaranteed him his job at the end of the war. Six hundred Guinness employees joined the British Army, a hundred of them never returning from the battlefields.

With 'Big Jim' Larkin away in the States, James Connolly, acting general secretary of the ITGWU, became more involved with Ireland's struggle for independence. On Easter Monday 1916 he was one of a group of idealistic rebels who led a short-lived rebellion and was one of fifteen leaders of that uprising to be killed by the British. Connolly had been seriously wounded during the fighting and was tied to a chair to prop him up in front of the British firing squad.

The insurrection was similar to the workers' defiance in supporting the ITGWU: it was another noble failure. While the Irish uprising was defeated, the brutality of the British in crushing it brought an international repulsion that led to the British government's acceptance of some form of independence for Ireland. The Irish Republican Army, a small but determined force, continued its battle against the might of Britain and declared independence by setting up its own parliament – the Dáil – in 1919.

Much has been written about Michael Collins and Eamon de Valera and the split created when Collins, in London negotiating on behalf of the Irish Republic, agreed a deal for partial Irish independence. Trade unionism, and the labour move- ment in general, was sidelined by the Civil War that followed. Brother turned against brother as the compromise of 'the Treaty' divided a new-born nation, the northern six counties remaining part of the United Kingdom.

Ireland was in a drastic economic state and Dublin was battered from the bombs and street battles of almost a decade of relentless turmoil by the time 'Big Jim' was out of American prison and back on the scene. He had received a pardon after serving three years in prison and was deported back to Ireland.

Larkin had a hero's welcome on his return to Dublin and immediately set about a tour of the country to meet his trade union members and to appeal for an end to the Civil War. He was still officially the general secretary of the ITGWU, but he had not grasped that things had changed in his long absence: one of his aides, William O'Brien, had become de facto leader of the union and had built it up from a membership of 5,000 to over 100,000. The union's motto, brought to Ireland from America by Connolly, of 'One Big Union' – OBU – had been adjusted by some to 'O'Brien's Union'. O'Brien had also become a key figure in the newly-combined Irish Labour Party and Trade Union Congress. A personality clash soon erupted between the two men – Larkin at one stage even suing O'Brien for libel and losing the case. There was not enough room in one union for these two egos. Sadly, both were vindictive and capable of ignoring all other consequences in pursuit of a vendetta.

'Big Jim' was expelled from the very trade union he had formed and O'Brien was promoted from general treasurer to general secretary. In response to this, Larkin's brother Peter (also no stranger to radicalism, having spent four years in prison in Australia for seditious conspiracy) set up the Workers' Union of Ireland with 'Big Jim' as its leader. It was a disaster for the trade union movement: two thirds of the ITGWU's Dublin membership transferred over to the WUI. Indeed, the ITGWU would see its membership collapse to less than 16,000 by the end of the decade while O'Brien swore to crush the WUI. Worse still, worker turned against worker: the Coal Merchants' Association locked out its ITGWU and WUI workers 'until a satisfactory guarantee is obtained that the men employed in the coal yards will work amicably together'. The WUI launched a mass attack on the ITGWU men at the North Wall. A bomb was thrown into a dock shed used by ITGWU workers, and WUI men even went to the homes of ITGWU men, intimidating their families. William 'Murder' Murphy would surely have been spinning with delight in his grave to see 'Larkin's rabble' divide and weaken.

And the divisions went deeper: Larkin shifted his attention to a political career and formed the pro-Communist Irish Workers' League which had the effect of dividing the left-wing vote between it and the O'Brien-led Irish Labour Party. The battle between these two men was one of the main reasons the Irish Labour movement never managed to become a significant voice or force in Irish politics in the nation's formative years.

O'Brien and Larkin continued to slug it out for the following two decades – they were well-matched in their capacity for carrying a grudge. In 1927 Larkin won a seat in the Dáil as an Independent Labour candidate. He was then removed because he was an 'undischarged bankrupt' – this as the result of the libel case he had taken and lost against O'Brien. A decade later Larkin won a seat again, though in one of the short-lived Dáils of that era, and he lost the seat the following year.

In the general election of June 1943 Larkin, by then a member of the Labour Party, again won a seat. This election marked another momentous event because now at Larkin's side was his eldest son, James Larkin Jr, who had also been elected to the Dáil. O'Brien, in response, withdrew his ITGWU from the Labour Party, saying it had been 'taken over by communists', and formed a separate National Labour Party. Once more, the Irish Labour movement paid the price for the endless brawl between these two ageing warhorses. 'Big Jim' Larkin's political success was again short-lived. In the general election of 1944 he lost his seat. His son, however, would remain a TD for twelve years.

When James Larkin Jr arrived in the Dáil – after two previous failed attempts – he was finally approaching some degree of equal status with his father even though he lived in the shadow of 'Big Jim' and was usually referred to, throughout his life, as 'Young Jim'. Larkin Jr, born in Liverpool in 1904, was one year old when his father lost his job as docker foreman. He was six when his father had his first stint in prison. Young James was sent to Scoil Éanna, the school run by brothers William and Padraig Pearse, but by 1914 the family moved to the USA where, six years later, his father was in prison facing a ten-year sentence. 'Big Jim' Larkin and his wife also separated when Larkin Jr was a young man. It was a turbulent upbringing and it must have been a formidable challenge to grow up as the eldest son and namesake of such an icon and firebrand. That said, he remained always at his father's side keeping with him all of his father's socialist conviction.

Young Jim was easily recognisable as his father's son: he was not quite as tall and not as heavily-built, but the facial features were quite similar – even if bespectacled Young Jim looked somewhat more bookish. The son was also as radical as his father; in 1928, he went to Moscow where he studied for two years at the Communist Academy, the Marx-Engels Institute and the Lenin Institute. On his return to Dublin he became assistant general secretary of the WUI while also developing his political career. There was a very strong bond between father and son – indeed, it has been noted that 'Big Jim' rarely mentioned any of his sons in writing other than 'Young Jim'.

For all the similarities, and the closeness, there was one crucial difference between father and son. The writer James Plunkett put it very succinctly in describing it as a difference of 'more mind and less mouth'. Unlike the father, the son was not a hot-head but was instead a clear and incisive thinker. As Assistant General Secretary of the WUI, he was the solid organising force behind his father's emotional chaos. Some were disappointed by his public speeches because he did not have the fire of his father. But those who actually dealt with him in negotiations admired his brilliance. He was highly regarded in the Dáil as a very effective politician, though he never made any attempt at holding power over the Labour Party that could have been considered almost his birthright. James Larkin Jr did not have his father's need to dominate.

The feud between Larkin and O'Brien triggered a final split: because Larkin was succeeding in his campaign to have the WUI included in the Irish Trade Union Congress, O'Brien's ITGWU, with eighteen other unions, withdrew from it and formed the Congress of Irish Unions.

Larkin's union was allowed into the ITUC shortly afterwards. O'Brien retired the following year, the rift between him and Larkin having overshadowed and diminished the Irish Labour movement for decades. Their personality clash had preoccupied the Labour movement in Ireland at a time when the struggling nation needed to see beyond the 'Civil War politics' of Fianna Fáil versus Fine Gael or other old foes.

On 30 January 1947 James Larkin died in his sleep. His health had been failing in previous years. He had lived a life driven by his belief in the working class, even if that was, at times, overshadowed by his difficult personality. Money was certainly never a motivation in his life. His biographer Emmet O'Connor wrote: 'Larkin left four pound ten shillings, the balance of his weekly wages, and a personal estate to the gross value of sixteen pound two shillings and sixpence.'

The outpouring of grief for 'Big Jim' across the country was immense. His body lay in state at the Thomas Ashe Hall for two days. Ireland was experiencing one of its worst winters on record yet many thousands of mourners showed up to walk through deep snow and blizzard conditions on Dublin's streets as Larkin's coffin was carried to Glasnevin Cemetery. O'Brien is said to have commented with typical bitterness: 'a showman to the last'.

On the day of his father's funeral James Jr published a letter in the *Irish Times*. At a time of national mourning – and with his rise to chief of the WUI imminent – he displayed a new, conciliatory approach. As he was standing at his father's graveside, the nation was reading Young Jim's words: he chose this emotional time not to score further points against political or trade union enemies but to call for unity in the Labour movement:

> With this great man's death, the last of the great figures of Irish Labour has passed, and we who remain are little people. If among those of us who occupy leading positions in the Labour movement there be individuals who, for one reason or another, represent obstacles or barriers to unity, let us grow in stature by stepping aside so that unity may be realised; if there are difficulties of policy standing in the way, let us, as we did this day, find the simplest common denominator in policy, and agree upon that as an immediate objective; if there are difficulties of organisation to overcome,

let us overcome them in the understanding that our organisations were built to serve Labour, not to shackle it.

James Larkin Jr TD inherited the role of secretary general of the Workers' Union of Ireland. It was the start of the shift of trade unionism in a manner his father had urged in a speech in 1923:

> Don't submit your mind to any one man. Think these problems out for yourselves. A leader who can lead you out of the wilderness can lead you back again. If there is a thinking intelligent movement, no leader can mislead you.

James Larkin Jr was the man to form such a 'thinking, intelligent movement'. As he sat behind his father's desk at the WUI headquarters in Thomas Ashe Hall he knew he was taking on a new set of challenges. He appointed John Smithers as General President of the union and Christy Ferguson as National Organiser. Ferguson was a man who was utterly devoted to the trade union movement. He was described in a trade union article, thought to have been written by Larkin, as: 'small in stature, a bundle of explosive energy, careful and painstaking in dealing with union members but clear and compelling in handling employers. Of course, he is not all perfection. Who is? He does not suffer fools gladly, insists upon clear and logical thinking and objects to being imposed upon by either union members or employers.' He would prove to be a key ally for Larkin.

Ferguson admired James Larkin Jr and wrote a perfect view on the comparisons made between father and son:

> In the early days of this century the unskilled and semi-skilled workers were exploited, down-trodden, without hope and without organisation. They needed a giant figure, a man with the courage of a lion and the voice of a trumpet to rouse them to their stature as men, not slaves. Old Jim, Big Jim Larkin, was the lion and the trumpet – the one man who could fulfil their deepest needs and lead them on the march.
>
> Now we need a skilled negotiator, rather than a fiery orator, a polished advocate, an intellectual with a brain as keen as a butcher's knife. We have these qualities in our General Secretary. In Dáil Eireann his speeches are seldom agitational; they are packed with

clear, concise thought, he reasons and by his use of pure reason he has become perhaps the most respected member of Dáil Eireann.

Larkin was known as a highly organised man, with a great understanding of the economy and of politics, respected throughout the Labour movement. Jack Harte recalled that: 'if any trade union official in the country got into trouble they went to Larkin.'

Probably not yet a priority – if even a consideration – for Larkin, was the prospect of the WUI becoming the recognised union for the general workers in Dublin's biggest and best employer: the Guinness Brewery. For its part, Guinness's would have been horrified at the thought of ever dealing with a work-force led by this radical son of an icon of labour agitation. They were Dublin's biggest employer. They produced what could indeed be described as Dublin's favourite product. The perfect employer, brewing the perfect pint, had reached the mid-1940s without having to deal with such troublesome matters as trade unionism. All this was about to change.

Three

Wanting a Voice

The fabled Arthur Guinness Son and Co, Ltd had been through many changes since the fiery days of the Dublin Lockout. Having dodged any ill-feeling from that drama they then kept on rolling out the Guinness barrels through the days of the War of Independence, the ensuing Civil War and the early days of the Irish Free State. Although the pint of plain was considered to be Dublin born and bred, when the Irish leader Eamon de Valera ventured into a trade war with Britain (one of his quotes being 'burn everything British but their coal') the Brewery was warned by the British that it could face high tariffs if it did not start brewing in Britain. A search began for a site for a new brewery and eventually an area named Park Royal, outside London, was chosen.

The notion that Guinness might be brewed anywhere other than at St James's Gate would fall somewhere between scandal and sacrilege, and when building began, it was done in secrecy: the companies named as developing the site were Agricultural Processes Ltd and the Park Royal Development Company. A man named Hugh Beaver led the development of the project for the construction company. The underlying instruction was that, despite the fact this development gave the opportunity to introduce modernisation, the new plant should be modelled on the 'medieval magic' of the St James's Gate brewery. Indeed, in keeping with that alchemy, shipments from the St James's Street brewery were sent over to mix with the Park Royal output to be sure the beloved Guinness taste standard was being maintained – until tests proved no taste difference between the British and Irish pint.

The plant, when up and running, became the seat of power of the Guinness company and the Dublin brewery became, in effect, a subsidiary. The Irish Minister for Industry and Commerce, Seán Lemass, was concerned when he was informed by Guinness's that the new plant was opening and was assured production in Dublin would not be reduced. But when war broke out Park Royal proved to be a crucial source of Guinness in Britain as any imports from Ireland came under possible German threat. Sales of Guinness in the coming years grew, with both breweries prospering and Park Royal producing twice the volume of Guinness as the Dublin brewery. Purists would always reckon, however, that Guinness produced in Dublin was the only true pint of plain.

Meanwhile back in Ireland, during 'The Emergency' that the rest of the world called World War Two, there had been a 'Standstill Order' on pay increases. This caused real wages to fall behind the cost of living throughout the country. There was great hardship for the Irish people and for the Irish nation as it lived through this war between giants on either side while remaining isolated. There was a high price to pay in trade and commerce for being a small island without allies.

In 1943, due to a problem with the vital supply of barley to the Brewery, Guinness suddenly dismissed five hundred of its non-skilled workers. Within a matter of weeks the men were re-hired when the problem was resolved. But the shock of the action left its mark and labourers realised how vulnerable they were to the decisions of those above them. The Guinness brewery was seen as a workers' paradise, but the general workers were realising that its 'Gods', as Jack Carruthers put it, could give and could take away as they chose.

In the new post-war world, in an Ireland with a divided and weak trade union movement, the Guinness non-trade workers took their first step towards organising. There had been an influx of new blood with the hiring of such men as Jack Harte and Jack Carruthers. These low-ranking and junior men had grievances and wanted these made known to their employers. However as the system then stood, they could report only to their foremen who were their immediate supervisors and who could find one way or another to shrug them off. The core issue was the paternalistic nature of the Guinness structure: management decided what was and was not good for the workers but had no interest in hearing their views. It was a case of Arthur knows best.

Somehow, among these hard-working men in the Brewery, their talk of discontent turned to action and a committee was formed which, in June 1946, issued a circular calling for Guinness non-trade workers to join the new Association of Brewery Employees. The Association quoted the view of Pope Leo XIII in his 1891 encyclical Rerum Novarum ('of new things') in which he set out a charter for moral behaviour between capital and labour. This urged the right of workers to form unions while rejecting the principles of communism. The encyclical stated: 'We lay it down as a general and lasting law that Working Men's Associations should be so organised and governed as to furnish the best and most suitable means for attaining what is aimed at: that is to say, for helping each individual member to better his condition to the utmost in body, soul and prosperity.'

The Association also quoted from the Vocational Organisation Report commissioned by Fianna Fáil in 1939: 'We recommend that in each industry Workers' Associations, corresponding as closely as possible with Employers' Associations, should be encouraged and promoted.' The report also specifically stated:'Employees of Messrs Guinness, who form the majority of the workers in the Industry (Brewing), are not organised. The Management of this firm does not object to the organisation of its workers.'

This circular was sent to management as well as to every employee. The Association was at pains to show respect to management. Chairman Michael Kiersey, Vice-Chairman Thomas Spollen and Honorary Secretary Peter Nevin, though all in their early thirties, had each been fifteen or more years with the company. This was not fiery rebellion but the voice of polite reason coming from a source never heard before: the bottom of the Brewery's pyramid structure. These men had started work in the Brewery as 'boys' and were already making their way up the grading system ladder. It was a conservative movement yet it was starting a huge change in the Brewery. Jack Harte was one of the first men to join the Association and from the beginning was active in supporting this move to give the non-trade workers a voice. Harte recalled: 'It gives emphasis by the fact that these guys were prepared to risk their positions. It meant that there was something really wrong.'

However, the old guard were quick to see the threat of all this. In the structure in Guinness as it stood, the non-skilled employees were kept under the control of the foremen. And it was the foremen who made the first move in response to the Association's circular: a deputation requested a meeting with senior management.

A Mr Heuston of the Registry Department (which nowadays would be called the personnel department) agreed on behalf of the Board to meet senior foremen Michael Farnan, James Breen, Thomas Glennon and Patrick Hughes. These men reported to him the unrest caused by the prospect of the forming of the Association. They said they were speaking on behalf of about two-thirds of the employees in stating: 'they do not think that any departure from the present system is necessary or desirable, as they know and appreciate that under it the best interests of the labouring staff have always and are continually receiving the attention of the Board.' They warned that the movement was coming mostly from the younger generation in the Brewery. Another point made by the deputation, and reported back to higher management by Heuston and his boss Morrissey, was very telling: 'They are of the opinion that direct access to the Board by the proposed Association in matters affecting employees would weaken the foremen's position and be detrimental to discipline.'

The foremen did not want the status quo disrupted. And as they were the only ones senior management or the Board had ever heard anyway, their word was taken as the truth of the situation. Writing later about these events, Sir Charles

Offley Harvey recalled that he discussed the situation with the then Managing Director, Lt. Colonel Charles Joseph Newbold. They agreed that: 'though everything should be done to restrain the activities of the Association it would be unwise to turn them down out of hand. Such action would merely drive them into the hands of a trade union which would not be to the advantage of the employees as a whole, embroiling them in trade disputes all over Ireland.'

Second Brewer Mr Cyril Buttanshaw was chairman of the Brewery's Labour Committee, which was a group of heads of department that acted in an advisory capacity to the Board on promotions and labour matters. He met a deputation from the Association on 19 July. It was surely a daunting event for the workers arriving in his office: the delegation was Kiersey, Nevin and a John Boyle of the Engineering Department. At that meeting, the Association delegates informed Buttanshaw that they had a membership of seven hundred. Buttanshaw said he could 'do nothing towards recognising them until they presented him with a list of members which he could scrutinise with a view to satisfying himself that they were representative of all employees.' Such was the state of communication between labourers and management in the Brewery. As long as the foremen were trusted and they assured management that all was well with the foot soldiers, there was no thought at Board level of any need for change – or, for that matter, any interest in change.

On 26 September, Buttanshaw again received a delegation from the Association. Their determination, like their numbers, had grown. Guinness had questioned the right of the Association to speak on behalf of the employees as they were not an officially-formed trade union. The Association were able to point out that they were an 'excepted body' in the terms of the 1941 Trade Unions Act as amended in 1942. They were: 'a body which carries on negotiations for the fixing of wages or other conditions of employment of its own members (but of no other employees).' Through this, the Association would later expand its name to 'The Association of Brewery Employees (Guinness)'. They reported, also, that their numbers had increased to 902. Buttanshaw maintained his previous position: he could do nothing until he saw the list of membership.

This took a month to organise, by which time membership had risen to 968 and the Association had held its inaugural general meeting and first elections. The Registry Department quickly set about a meticulous analysis of the membership list. The management wanted to know exactly what they were being confronted with. Percentages of membership were broken down by grades, departments and age: it showed that few employees in higher positions or over the age of fifty had joined. As the deputation of foremen had pointed out, the senior men in the Brewery had no interest in the Association and very few men in the higher non-trade grades joined it (none at all in the Grades 1 and 1A). The largest percentage were in the Tariff (general labourer) or Temporary category: precisely the men with least access to a say in their working lives and precisely the men management had never spoken with. The overall percentage of membership in non-trade workers was 41 percent. It should have been more than enough to be recognised as a voice bringing a new era in Guinness industrial relations. The problem was that the management plainly felt this development was not a matter to be taken seriously.

Guinness never behaved in an anti-union manner and were worthy of their high reputation as employers. But the smugness of the almost two-hundred-year-old company in how it was structured and how highly it was regarded as an employer made it blind to changes sweeping the modern world in workers' rights. Having established the Association's membership level and profile the Board felt it was insignificant. They decided to deal with it only through Buttanshaw, who wrote a letter to the Association, dated 25 October 1946, that was little more than a brush-off informing them that the Board: 'have authorised me to receive direct any suggestions or complaints employees may wish to make. . . . I shall be willing to receive a delegation whenever you have a general question to bring forward, but I cannot accept you as speaking for all the employees of the Brewery, nor as the sole channel of approach.'

As a perfect contrast to this and an insight to industrial relations in the Brewery at that time, Buttanshaw issued a letter to the Manager of the Registry Department four days later in which he instructed that, as a result of representations made to him by the men in No.1 and No.1a Grades: 'The Board wish as much as is reasonably possible to be done to increase the standing of these grades. . . . They should not have to take their turn with the other men for payment of wages but should receive them separately. They should be passed in at once when attending at the Dispensary. They should have a table reserved for them at luncheon in the Workmen's Rooms. They should not have to check in and out in the ordinary way, but should sign a book or, at any rate, have their attendance checked by some method other than that used for the other men.'

It was clear that the old ways were holding firm.

But the October letter from Buttanshaw had, in its opening line, a comment that baffled the executive of the Association: 'In the Brewery Rules of Employment (Rule 3 last paragraph) it is already established that any general complaints or requests of employees shall be represented to the Board.' This was the first time these men had heard of rules governing their employment! Men with several decades of experience had never known or seen these 'Brewery Rules of Employment'. The committee sent a deputation to Buttanshaw requesting a copy of the rules and he said he could have a copy typed up for them. The following afternoon he called the deputation back to inform them that the Rules were not for circulation: no one below the level of manager could have a copy. These men were living under rules they did not even have the privilege of reading.

Perhaps, after this, the Association began to see what they were facing. The leaders of the Association were undaunted, however, and their numbers were continuing to grow. In November they rented offices at 14 Thomas Street near the Brewery. Days before Christmas they held a general meeting, at the Mansion House, that produced their agenda for the changes they sought. They were looking for sweeping increases of wages across their grades. Sir Charles Harvey, later writing about their demands in a management memo, described them as exorbitant.

In the meantime, there had been developments across the shore in Park Royal. Managing director Newbold died suddenly and Rupert Guinness replaced him with a man already stationed at the ailing managing director's side: Sir Hugh Eyre Campbell Beaver. Beaver was the first man to take on this job who had come from a non-brewery background, but he had been knighted for his outstanding achievements running the Ministry of Works during the war and he had, like Harvey, been brought into the Guinness fold. He had also overseen the construction of Park Royal. Beaver was a highly-regarded leader and an article about him quoted this exchange: 'Someone once said to him "Why can't you leave well enough alone?" Sir Hugh's instant rejoinder was "Because well won't leave itself alone".' Beaver and Harvey would prove to be a very dynamic match in managerial style and in vision.

Perhaps an unfortunate coincidence for the Association was that their meeting on 22 December fell days before the Board held a meeting at which it decided to revise wage rates in the Brewery. When the 'Standstill Order' was lifted in September 1946, the Brewery cancelled a 'bonus' system they had been using to negate its impact on the workers and raised the basic rate from sixty-six shillings a week to eighty-six shillings a week. In late December they raised the rate again to one hundred shillings a week: a cumulative raise of 50 percent. This might have seemed like a fine gesture in the Guinness tradition, but this in fact still didn't bring wages up to their pre-war level when adjusted for the rising cost of living. The Board must have felt, however, that these pay rises should have calmed the workers down.

In a letter dated 29 January 1947, Honorary Secretary Peter Nevin wrote to Buttanshaw on behalf of the Association informing him of the General Meeting of the previous month and: 'in view of the power unanimously conferred upon the Executive Committee by the general body at that meeting, I hereby submit on behalf of our 1,310 members the following recommendations for consideration by the Board: . . .'

The letter went on to outline a string of pay increases for the Grades 2 to 5 that the Association represented: raises in rates for shift and night work, raises in rates paid for overtime on Sunday, Saturday ('short') day or after three hours overtime already worked. The letter ended with a restrained hint of the frustrations of the men: 'I also wish to point out that the limited recognition accorded to the Association is not regarded as satisfactory, and would request that the Board reconsider their decision and acknowledge this Association to deal with Departmental matters.'

The following day, 'Big Jim' Larkin, died. On 2 February, in exceptional blizzard conditions for Ireland, there was a memorial Mass for Larkin celebrated by Archbishop McQuaid and then the funeral procession to Glasnevin cemetery. The *Irish Press* listed the representatives at the funeral from the many Irish trade unions. On the list were Messrs Brady, Kiersey and Prior from the Association. This newspaper clipping was archived by the Guinness personnel department, with an 'x' marked beside the reference to the Association.

On 5 February, Buttanshaw met a deputation from the Association, but a letter from him to the Association a few days later plainly and bluntly closed the door: 'Your letter is concerned with the rates of wages and hours of work. Messrs Arthur Guinness Son and Co Ltd are regarded as the best employers in this country, and the Board periodically review the rates of pay and conditions of employment to ensure that not only do they fulfil the requirements of the law, but also remain in advance of other firms. . . . The Board does not, therefore, intend at this stage to make any change, but all matters affecting the welfare of their employees are under the Board's continual consideration.'

A memorandum about the Association written by the new head of Guinness Sir Hugh Beaver, based in the Park Royal Guinness brewery, summed up the ongoing development of strategy in dealing with the Association. He stated that: 'it would be far more satisfying to be dealing with a Union with wider interests, even though that obviously involved some obvious disadvantages in other directions.' He was also interested in a card that would later be played in this game of strategies: 'The Dublin Board will consider the desirability of having some sort of Works Committee. In a Works Committee this Association would be represented but it would only be there with representatives and members of other Unions and the Management is, of course, equally represented. Normally Works Committees will not deal with questions of wages; that is obvious and necessary in England because there are Unions to deal with all such questions. In the absence of stable and influential Unions in Ireland the position is less simple.' For whatever reason – that would well have interested Jack Carruthers working in that department – Beaver noted also that: 'In any such Committee the Coopers, in the Dublin Board's view, should remain outside.'

Beaver also anticipated that the Association's next step would be to go to the Labour Court. In fact, that was not the Association's next move. They instead wrote back to Buttanshaw in April a two-page letter signed by Honorary Secretary Nevin. They asked the Board to reconsider its position 'in view of the modern trend in industrial relationships'. He wrote:

> 'My Committee is particularly concerned with the Board's proposal to limit the activities of the Association to matters of general interest, thus excluding purely Departmental affairs. This attitude on the part of the Board, if persisted in, would render the Association ineffective in respect to its most fundamental object, i.e. the provision of a direct contact between the Board of Directors and the employees. It is considered unfair to place the onus of redressing a grievance on the individual who may, for good reasons, be unwilling to take action on his own behalf.'

Harvey and Beaver were monitoring the correspondence being exchanged between the Association and Buttanshaw. They were taking the matter seriously – but remained unsure how to react. A management summit meeting was held in Dublin on 1 May 1947 'to discuss the question of forming a Works Committee at St James's Gate'. Senior Guinness figures such as Lord Moyne (Bryan Walter Guinness) and J. A. Webster had come over from Park Royal. Harvey and

Buttanshaw were among the senior figures attending from the Dublin brewery. The minutes of the meeting reveal as fine a conspiratorial exchange as one could hope to find in any high-level political intrigue. It is a perfect snapshot of the shock to the Guinness system when this league of gentlemen was confronted by the possible rise of organised labour.

Webster opened the meeting by reporting Beaver's view on the idea of setting up a Works Committee at St James's Gate. There had been discussions about the possibility of having a Works Committee in Park Royal, but no decision had yet been made. Beaver had been advised by some government departments that Works Committees were the rule in England and not the exception. Shop stewards in Park Royal were already forming their own Committee and might bring pressure on management to do the same. Beaver felt that although Park Royal managed without a Works Committee, the running of the company might have been smoother through the war years if one had existed. As a Works Committee seemed likely to be established in Park Royal, Beaver concluded, it seemed illogical not to have one in Dublin.

But the general mood at this meeting was against the formation of a Works Committee: 'It was felt that a Works Committee was, as in the case of the Association of Brewery Employees, contrary to the Guinness spirit, but that we should have to have something of the kind in a few years when the older men had been replaced by a younger generation.' The sentiment was that the establishing of a Works Committee would open Pandora's Box: it could encourage the workers to join the Association which in turn could create frustrations as wages and hours of work could not be discussed and this could in turn 'drive the employees into the arms of Trade Unions and thereby involve them in strikes in sympathy with dockers and transport workers'.

Webster asked what was the likely growth of trade unionism among the general labourers. Buttanshaw replied that he thought 'the Unions do not want our men as our rates of pay were so much higher than those of any other firm'.

Strategies were then discussed about how to deal with the Association's wishes as expressed in their April letter. Webster proposed sticking with the line as drawn in the October 1946 Guinness letter: 'deal with the Association in the same way as we do with any other groups of employees who have complaints to make'. Buttanshaw suggested making lines of approach to him or to heads of department as easy as possible so that there would be no need for the Association. Sir Charles Harvey 'suggested that Mr Buttanshaw should receive a deputation from the Association and ask them why they want to raise departmental matters and, in general, let them blow off steam. This suggestion received the support of Mr Webster.'

Webster summed up the general opinion of the meeting. The Association could raise matters (not including wages or working hours) 'in a small deputation of members' within a department or, if it were an inter-departmental issue, they could go to Mr Buttanshaw.

In conclusion: 'It was decided that Mr Buttanshaw should see the Secretary of the Association and inform him that the Board were not prepared to alter the arrangement conveyed to the Association in Mr Buttanshaw's letter of 25th October, 1946; that foremen will be notified that they are to facilitate as much as possible any man who wishes to see the head of his department at any time. He would also point out the benefits enjoyed by our employees over those of other firms.'

There was a significant coda to the meeting: 'Buttanshaw asked if the Board wished him to give way on any point, but a decision on this was postponed to a later date'. The Board wanted to see how the Association would react before they would consider any thoughts of giving ground.

Buttanshaw, sticking to the script as agreed at the summit meeting, had another cordial but fruitless meeting with a delegation from the Association in early May. The atmosphere in the room must have been extremely icy. The men reiterated their right to an increase in wages to match the rise in the cost of living. Buttanshaw reminded them that Guinness provided great security and many benefits. 'I do not think they really hoped for any increase in wages as a result of their letter,' he wrote in his report back to the Board on the meeting. He also expressed exactly the blinkered managerial view that the labourers were trying to change – the paternalism of the company:

> Turning to the question of non-recognition of the Association as regards departmental matters, I said that the Board would deprecate any departure from the procedure laid down in my letter of the 25 October, 1946, in the case of complaints and requests by individuals. They considered that these could be dealt with as in the past through Heads of Departments, who bear a kind of paternal relationship to employees in their Departments – the Guinness tradition. To remove any fear of obstruction by foremen, instructions are being issued that no obstacle is to be put in the way of any man approaching the Head of Department and that no reason must be asked for.

The delegation asked if a representative of the Association could accompany an employee at such a meeting with a Head of Department. To copper-fasten the freeze-out, Buttanshaw replied that someone could do so – provided he was concerned with the matter being brought up and was not present as a representative of the Association.

The velvet gauntlet had been thrown down. It was decision time for the Association. Their response was a polite letter expressing disappointment with the meeting – though noting that Buttanshaw was always courteous when they met – and assuring management that they would never bother them with 'trifling matters'. They stated that they would hold a special general meeting to present the situation to their members. By now, management probably felt that the strategy agreed the previous October was working: restraining the Association without turning it down out of hand – hoping, presumably, that it would run out of steam.

June 1947. It was the anniversary of the distributing of the circular announcing the birth of the Association. A special general meeting was called for noon on the 22nd Sunday at O'Connell Hall, 42 Upper O'Connell Street. The Executive Committee broke the news to those assembled of the impasse with management.

The outcome was a resolution to inform Guinness that: 'if the Board persisted in its continued refusal to accede to the Association's request to act on behalf of its members both individually and collectively, the Association would have no alternative but to seek the services of the Labour Court in this matter'.

The Irish Labour Court had been established in 1946 as part of the Industrial Relations Act. Its aim was to be an intermediary between employer and employee, and it consisted of a chairman plus two representatives from each side of this divide. It was considered a place where compromise could be reached between employer and employee. The whole concept had been set up by Seán Lemass in an attempt to centralise the trade union situation in Ireland with its two congresses and two major unions: both situations the outcome of the split between Larkin and O'Brien. Lemass hoped to see the elimination of the left-leaning WUI and of those remaining unions in Ireland affiliated to England.

In the struggle between Guinness and the Association the Labour Court certainly seemed like the logical way to find a solution. The prospect of being brought to the Labour Court did not, at first, phase the Guinness management. Harvey sent a memo to Buttanshaw in response to the Associations July letter in which he simply stated that 'the Board see no reason to alter the decision given in their letter to you of 30 May, 1947'. The two sides prepared their cases. For some reason, in the lead up to the Court hearing, the Guinness management became unnerved. The Association had been requesting from management details about pre-war wages and the Court had been asking management for details about the Association. Then management asked the Association to send it copies of its correspondence with the Labour Court which the Association duly provided. Harvey then sent a letter to the Labour Court informing them of wage increases already given to the employees. T. J. Cahill of the Labour Court wrote to Harvey: 'The information given in your letter has been noted, though the Court is somewhat at a loss to understand how a letter addressed by it to the Association of Brewery Employees should be the occasion of a communication from the Board of your Company.'

The hearing was on 27 February 1948 in the Labour Court on South Circular Road. It was the first time that the two sides would, in principle at least, face each other as equals. Each had thoroughly prepared their cases.

John Boyle presented the case for the Association, the membership of which had grown to 1,507 men. He read out a prepared five-page outline written 'without help from either Lawyer or Trade Union'. The statement gave a history of the body's founding, the frustrations caused by the lack of communication and being brushed off by the Brewery management despite the employees' wish for good relations with their employers. His words were eloquent and heartfelt, if still subservient:

> A Manager in the Brewery has absolutely no direct contact with the men in his Department, due to the large numbers involved he does not and cannot be expected to know even their names, much less their ability or character. Consequently, he has to rely solely on information given to him by overseers or foremen when requiring knowledge of any man. It is therefore obvious that a man has to look to those over him for a favourable recommendation to his Manager. It naturally follows that this one-sided channel of the authorities for gaining knowledge concerning any man can be, and we definitely state has been, subject to abuse and men have found when attempting to voice some particular complaint which may specifically concern them, that information regarding themselves has already been placed before the Authorities without their knowledge, and if they challenged it they did so without avail and to their disadvantage.

He concluded:

> It is not our policy to embarrass our employer by airing to this Court the many grievances under which our fellow workers suffer, though if the Court deems it necessary we shall willingly supply and prove further facts in this respect. The majority of employees of Messrs A. Guinness, Son & Co Ltd, are convinced after nearly thirty years experience of the unsatisfactoriness of the present system that it is necessary for them to be able to place facts and information before their employers by means of elected representatives elected by the whole body of the workers and voice, not imaginary or frivolous grievances, but concrete cases. This double

channel for the authorities and employees would facilitate both parties, thereby reducing discontent and dissatisfaction and it would remove from the individual fear of antagonising his overseers in trying to redress his own complaints.

In conclusion may I say that very many people in this country think that the labouring men employed by Guinness work under ideal conditions; no doubt we enjoy some facilities of which we are not unappreciative, but we, the workers, and if I may say, the consumers of the product, should be the best judge. Men in some departments work under conditions which we venture to state would be rectified immediately if they were members of some Union, or if this Association was permitted to place their grievances before the Board.

Morrissey read the position of the Guinness management from a document drawn up by Sir Charles Harvey. It began with a statement that came as a surprise to the representatives of the Association: 'Messrs Arthur Guinness Son and Co Ltd have no objection whatsoever to carrying on negotiations with a recognised Trade Union, and indeed they already deal with the various Unions to which the Tradesmen belong. The non-tradesmen employees in the firm, with perhaps a few exceptions, do not belong to a Trade Union.' The statement went on to give a summary of the history of the Association, belittling it by noting that: 'the mere fact that the annual subscription to this Association is only two shillings shows that the Association has no responsibilities of a serious nature.'

The statement concluded by reiterating the Guinness pride in being 'amongst the best employers in the country': 'The Board are constantly reviewing their conditions and terms of employment and are satisfied that those which the Company offers compare very favourably with those that are to be found elsewhere. This is borne out by the fact that there have never been any serious disputes between the management and its employees. The Board therefore are reluctant to take any line of action which might upset the existing harmony'.

A harmony, of course, that was a fiction told by the foremen and lower management to their superiors all the way up to the Board – who were happy to believe the lie.

According to Harvey's report back to Beaver, what followed next was confusion among the Association deputation. The Court asked Harvey and Morrissey to leave the room and had a private conversation with the Association delegates. On Harvey and Morrissey's return twenty minutes later the Chairman of the Court said the case would be adjourned indefinitely, hopefully never to return to the Labour Court, because the representatives of the Association wanted to go back to their members to find out if they wanted to join a trade union.

Harvey wrote to Beaver: 'I think we can regard this settlement as fairly satisfactory and hope that we shall now be able to settle this domestic squabble by means of a little private conversation with the leaders of the Association.'

Having beaten the movement, Guinness management were quick to move in with salve to soothe any bruises. A company notice was issued to 'The non-tradesmen Employees of St James's Gate Brewery'. It summarised the outcome of the Labour Court hearing and reassured the workers 'the Board consider the existing arrangements in the Brewery are adequate to keep them fully informed on the terms and conditions of employment and on any matters which an employee or group of employees may wish to raise'. It reiterated the Board's view that it had no objection to men joining a recognised trade union, yet stated: 'The Board are also satisfied that under the existing arrangements and system in the Brewery the terms and conditions of employment, the opportunities for advancement, the security of employment and the measure of social security offered to the employees of the Company are more favourable than are to be found elsewhere. This statement is confirmed by the few resignations from the Company's service which take place, and by the long list of candidates awaiting an opportunity of entering the Company's service.'

Harvey asked Buttanshaw and Morrissey to contact the Association for a meeting with a deputation to ask what their next move would be. In this request, Harvey showed that the management's stated openness to a trade union representing the men was indeed a strategy: 'The Board are determined that no man shall be forced to join a Trade Union against his will and without his eyes open. You should emphasise that a man has always had the right to join a Trade Union if he so desires, but it never has been a condition of employment in this firm that a man must join one. It is entirely a matter of free choice for the individual concerned. The Board feel that there are very many men who are satisfied with the existing arrangements and who would be reluctant to join a Trade Union with its outside connections and responsibilities unless they were persuaded to do so by a one-sided representation of the actual state of affairs.'

The meeting with the Association was very subdued. The deputation stated that they were considering changing from an association to a trade union but had not yet reached a decision in response to the Labour Court outcome and had nothing to say until there had been a meeting of the executive committee. A further meeting was held between management and representatives of the Association (Kiersey, Nevin and Boyle) at the end of the month. At this, a representative of the Association read out a statement which announced that there would be a general meeting on 13 April at which both cases, as presented to the Court, would be presented to the members. The Association were plainly still in disarray, stating: 'The Court in adjourning this case were under the impression that the company wanted the men to join a Union and, further, that here was a situation where we were trying to get in the thin end of the wedge and the employer came along and gave it a tremendous whack.' The men promised to contact management before announcing any decision and reiterated their belief that acceptance of the Association would be better for both sides than bringing in an outside union. Buttanshaw, reporting back on this meeting, concluded by reporting: 'Mr Morrissey and I think that they feel they are in a very difficult position and are anxious about the future of the Association. We think that any further recognition would be unwise, and would give them a new lease of life.'

Meanwhile, Harvey was drafting a notice that would be issued to all employees before the upcoming general meeting of the Association. In a perhaps unusual, certainly strategic, move the management called in a deputation of the Association to show them the contents before its release to the general staff.

The notice, to 'Non-tradesmen employees on the ordinary list of St James's Gate Brewery', summarised the events of the Labour Court hearing and stated that the Board had no objection to any employees joining a union ('but it must be remembered that Trade Unions have responsibilities and connections outside the Brewery, and every man should consider the matter deeply from all its aspects before making his decision'). Harvey also announced what had already been discussed internally and adopted at the Park Royal plant: the setting up of a Works Committee. This committee would have no more than a quarter of its members appointed by the Board with the rest being elected representatives of the employees. It would not be able to negotiate rates of pay or conditions of employment, but would be an open line of communication between management and employees on all matters of mutual welfare.

At the meeting, the deputation were given the option of proposing to their members at the general meeting that the Works Committee idea be supported: 'It was pointed out to them that they would be able to claim that they had achieved the main object for which the Association was formed – that of getting the Management into closer touch with representatives of the employees.'

The deputation went away to discuss the situation with the Association's executive committee. They returned to management the following day and, as Buttanshaw wrote in his report on the meeting, 'made efforts to keep the Association in the limelight, by asking that they should be allowed to take an active part in the setting up of the Works Committee.' This was not agreed, but in the end the notice was slightly altered – mentioning that discussions had been held with the Association – so they could get some credit from the new development. It was a small and patronising gesture, management by now clearly feeling they had the upper hand. The men forming and leading the Association were out of their depth, still caught in their serfdom frame of mind.

Harvey was keeping Beaver informed of developments and wrote: 'Carlyle and I discussed the matter very fully with heads of departments, and also with the Chairman and Vice-Chairman. We feel it would be a mistake to take any action that would drive the men into the hands of a Trade Union. Though at the moment probably no more than one hundred or so would join, yet there is no doubt that a few would, and that would be the thin end of the wedge which would become driven very quickly'.

On 20 April, Kiersey, Nevin and Boyle returned to inform management that the resolution at the general meeting recommending the Works Committee was passed by a very large majority. They said also that there was a wish among members that the Association continue to exist. Buttanshaw reported that at his meeting with the deputation they told him: 'The executive committee had made it clear at the meeting that the Association was not a Trade Union and that it never had been the intention to usurp the function of a Trade Union; and they had pointed out the dangers of the infiltration of Trade Unions amongst the workers in the Brewery.' The bogey-man notion of trade unionism had clearly now been instilled in the Association's representatives.

Reporting this meeting to Sir Hugh Beaver, Sir Charles Harvey wrote: 'This is all quite satisfactory, and I doubt whether we shall hear much more from the Association'.

Harvey presented the constitution for the Works Committee in May 1948. It was truly a tamed voice for the workers, its main aim established as being 'to facilitate consultation between the management and personnel of the company on matters of common interest'. It was trade unionism on the employer's terms: a committee of twelve, of whom only four would be 'non-tradesmen' even though the majority of Guinness employees were 'non-tradesmen'. No one less than five years in the company's employ was eligible to join the committee (so excluding the younger workers it was felt had started the trade unionism movement in the brewery). Rules were set down as to what the Works Committee could and could not discuss (even down to stating it could not 'interfere in matters which are already covered by existing organisations such as the Guinness Athletics Union or the Workmen's Rooms Committee'). Meetings would happen once every second month. Members of the Board of Directors were free to sit in on the committee's meetings whenever they wished. Harvey wrote that the Committee's function would be: 'advisory and will include discussions on any matters affecting the health, comfort and happiness of the employees and the general efficiency of the Brewery'.

All was back to normal. Or so it seemed. Harvey had reported to Beaver that the Association had been dealt with when they accepted the Works Committee structure. A year later, the Association called a meeting of its members – 'the most vitally important since the formation of the Association'. The executive committee were going to propose that the Association be disbanded and that its members join a trade union.

After the Labour Court hearing, Harvey had smugly described the matter as 'settled'. Far from being settled, however, the matter would now open onto a far wider arena. Guinness had made a gambit when they stated to the Labour Court that they would prefer to work with an experienced trade union. Guinness was the trade union jewel in the crown. There were many unions out there that would give their eye teeth to represent its non-tradesmen employees. In particular, this would become a new battleground for the ongoing rivalry between the ITGWU and the WUI. Big Jim's son was about to make his presence felt in the Guinness boardroom. And it was here Sir Charles Harvey would discover what is was like to sit opposite a brilliant and determined voice for the workers in the Guinness brewery.

Four

Larkin at the Gates

Peter Nevin's comments on the agendas of two meetings of the Works Committee (January and March 1949) survive in the Irish Labour History Society archives. Down along the items proposed he has pencilled such comments as 'long finger', 'no', 'no change', 'petered out', 'to be considered'. Not a single item from the two agendas – most of the proposals were trivialities such as facilities for smoking at work or for having a suggestion box – were agreed and initiated. Guinness management had painted the Association of Brewery Employees into a corner: one voice on the multi-layered all-department Works Committee that wanted the Guinness hierarchy to live long and prosper.

Some on the executive committee of the Association found the situation acceptable but, three years after the Association had been established and had set out to be recognised by the Board, enough of its committee were able to win a vote for the radical proposal of offering the membership the option of disbanding the Association and joining a trade union. This led to the Association committee doing some shopping around as they considered which trade union to join. There were small unions, such as the National Union of Vintners', Grocers' and Allied Trades' Assistants, that were possibilities but the two main choices were, of course, the ITGWU or the WUI. The latter would be the most radical choice, having links to socialism and the extreme left.

But when the committee's delegation met James Larkin they were greatly impressed by him. Jack Harte, though not at that meeting, recalled that Young Larkin's personality and intelligence was the deciding factor in winning over the Association: they could see that with him they would have the perfect leader for the challenges that lay ahead. They saw in him a match for the Brewery management and Board. One can imagine that when they told him their tale of getting the run-around from Buttanshaw and being pigeon-holed for what they could and could not talk about he leaned forward in his father's chair and explained to them the strategies that were being played out. He certainly opened their eyes.

In what was surely a dreadful piece of bad luck or bad timing for the ITGWU, a deputation from the Association also sought a meeting with Frank Robbins, Secretary of the union's Dublin District Council, but he was away in the USA. The Association of Brewery Employees called their general meeting to vote on which union to join. Already convinced after their meeting with Larkin, the Association's Executive Committee would be recommending the Workers' Union of Ireland.

There was a scatter of activity as a wave of turmoil swept through the Brewery. The Guinness brewery was in danger of swinging from one extreme to another: from benign employer not having a trade union representing its non-trade workers, to besieged employer having to cope with the radical left-wing union of Jim Larkin. As the agenda for the special general meeting became known, the Irish Transport and General Workers' Union geared up for a response. The result was, as the brewery men arrived for the meeting, an ITGWU circular was handed out to them addressed to 'The Employees of Arthur Guinness & Co.'

The document encouraged the workers to unionise, stating: 'workers generally in every walk of life, and in almost every country in the world, have long since made up their minds that it is only through Trade Union organisation and efficient Trade Unionism, can the justice which is theirs, and their rights be maintained'. It then went on to summarise the many reasons why they should join the ITGWU: the scale and experience of the union; the range of industries it represented; the number of branches throughout Ireland north and south.

The union could boast: 'It has at its command through its organisation of Transport, Dock and Air Workers, an effective weapon in the event of strike action being forced upon any of its members'. There were a few little swipes at the WUI: James Larkin was an elected TD in the Irish Dáil but the document boasted that the ITGWU had five representatives in Dáil Eireann and a senator, too. The final paragraph aired the old rivalry between the two unions: 'The Union has no outside Ireland affiliations and it is satisfied that neither the economic nor the industrial life of our people can be adversely affected or dominated in any way by its affiliations, and it is with this confidence and the full knowledge of our responsibilities in this matter we suggest that you should become organised in a Trade Union, and that the Union best fitted for you is the Irish Transport and General Workers' Union.'

The special general meeting of the Association of Brewery Employees was set for noon, Sunday 29 May, in the Supper Room of the Mansion House. Both Harte and Carruthers were at the meeting. A circular had been sent out addressed to every member of the Association, but word of the importance of the impending meeting spread to all employees. Harvey, showing that he was not keeping a neutral stance in all this, informed Beaver: 'We are doing our best to ensure that the meeting is well attended so that whatever resolutions are passed may be reasonable'. The result of all this expectation and concern was chaos.

The room booked could hold no more than six hundred and was soon overfull with many members of the Association unable to gain entry. The Chairman called for all those who were not members of the Association to leave the room. But a circular issued in the brewery earlier in the week had given the impression that all non-tradesmen were welcome. The *Irish Independent* reported that the Chairman's call: 'caused vigorous protest, and a large body of Association members left with the non-members'. There was huge disruption as this human traffic moved back and forth. Kiersey said the Association's committee decided they should join a trade union because the Guinness Board 'refused to recognise the

Association as a responsible body'. Then Christy Ferguson, national organiser of the Workers' Union of Ireland, presented the case for joining his union.

An *Irish Press* account of the meeting makes for very colourful reading. Before Ferguson could speak, a man from the audience climbed up onto the platform and declared that a member of the executive committee 'had justified the terrible sentence and imprisonment of Cardinal Mindszenty.' Mindszenty was the head of the Catholic Church in Hungary and an anti-Communist who had been tortured and, in a show trial just months before this meeting, had been sentenced to life in prison. Mr J. Brady, a trustee of the Association, demanded that the remark 'Communist' be withdrawn and an apology given but the man who had made the accusation left the hall 'throwing his membership card on the floor'.

Plainly, the mood of the executive committee had changed. From going cap-in-hand in the early days seeking recognition from Guinness management, they were now proposing that their members join a union whose representative Christy Ferguson (who, like James Larkin Jr had studied in Moscow), announced to the Guinness workers: 'The Workers' Union of Ireland has a record of strikes second to none. There may come days again when strikes will be the only argument which may be used.'

After Ferguson gave his speech the Chairman, Michael Kiersey, asked for a show of hands to decide if the Association would disband and its members join the WUI. A man in the audience shouted out: 'You are putting a gun to our heads to join one union.' The newspaper reported: 'The man left amid uproar and was followed by others'.

Reports differ as to what happened next and Kiersey would write to the *Irish Independent* days later stating that the meeting had been completely orderly. When Harvey, presumably informed by a secret observer, was writing a memo to Beaver about events he stated that by the time the matter came to a vote there were only a few hundred men in the room and the outcome was so narrow that those for and against had to stand at opposite sides of the room so that a head count could be done. Harvey wrote: 'A lot more of those who were against then left, and probably no more than 150 were present when the final vote was taken'.

The vote was in favour of joining the union. The committee of the Association, with Kiersey as Chairman, dissolved and became that of the Guinness branch of the WUI. Another report was that, while all this drama was going on, six hundred Guinness workers had moved elsewhere when they could not get into the meeting and had voted en masse to join the WUI.

The fall-out from that Sunday in the Mansion House spread like wildfire through the Brewery. The old ways were under siege and all was in uproar. Shop floor, union offices and management all jumped into action. Larkin was at St James's Gate.

Having sailed quietly through the labour turbulence of decades, the Brewery was suddenly being hit by a tidal wave.

Jack Carruthers was one of the many unconvinced by the exodus to the WUI and became part of a counter-movement instantly set up by a non-trades Foreman named Carrick: the Guinness Employees' Organisation. It was odd that Jack Carruthers would join this movement, but Jack Harte said he believed Carruthers was being influenced by a foreman he had become friendly with. This new grouping held on to the belief that it would be better for the labourers to have an in-house alliance rather than be involved with trade unionism at large. And so, on the day after the Sunday meeting of the Association, yet another circular was being passed to the men in the Brewery: this time, by the quickly-formed Employees' Plebiscite Committee. It presented the simple question 'Do you wish to join a Union? YES or NO.' The committee asked Guinness management, via Buttanshaw, to help in the arranging of this plebiscite but when Harvey was approached about this he declined, writing: 'The Board feel that this is a matter in which the management cannot interfere.'

A figure of 2,200 ballot papers were issued of which 1,257 were returned: 1,047 were against joining a trade union. Guinness management were, of course, very pleased to learn of this outcome. But it was precisely an exercise in what had caused the build up of resentment over the years on the factory floor. Two variations of the ballot had been distributed – all by Guinness foremen during their work shifts. Both variations were on Guinness official letterhead and one, with an extra touch of intimidation, even had each worker's company number. In the Brewery's hierarchy of the time, the threat was very thinly veiled. One can imagine a worker's foreman walking up to him with this ballot paper with its blunt question – the clear unspoken message would be that how the man voted would decide his work circumstances for a long time to come. The foremen were not going to tolerate any usurping of their position as the wall between the non-tradesmen and the management 'gods'.

The result of the plebiscite was a boost for the newly-formed Guinness Employees' Organisation. Management were against this, however, saying that the Works Committee was still the best way of maintaining open communication with non-trade employees. But two significant concessions were offered: the Works Committee could raise matters of wages and conditions, and departmental sub-committees could be set up to reduce the gap between management and staff. This was what the Association had been seeking for three years. It had come a week too late.

The ITGWU, meanwhile, launched a counter-attack against the WUI, seeing the jewel in the trade union crown being grabbed from under its nose. It issued a circular to all Guinness employees on 3 June in which it stated that a letter written to the Association more than a week before the May general meeting had not been passed on to the members. They reproduced that letter, in which they apologised for the missed opportunity for representatives of the Association to meet Frank Robbins and offered to meet representatives 'on any date and at any time to suit your convenience, when we shall give you full details regarding this organisation'.

The ITGWU was the sensible choice for the Guinness non-tradesmen. The letter could list all the similar workers it represented and stated: 'It is at least ten times larger than any other union and, indeed, its membership equals that of all other working-class organisations combined'. It already represented brewery workers in such counties as Cork, Kilkenny and Tipperary. It emphasised alliances, through the Congress of Irish Unions, to relevant unions such as the Regular Dublin Coopers' Society. It gave details of its financial assets and the support and benefits it offered. The letter concluded by stating that Guinness employees could transfer from the Association to the union 'as full benefit members'. But no movement in the Brewery built up around this. The WUI had already stolen its rival's march.

James Larkin was making his own move. He called for a special meeting of the 'Brewery (Guinness's) Section of the WUI' on 9 June at which he would address the 'members and intending members'. He was presumably only then made aware of the plebiscite and how it had been conducted because the following day he shot off an angry letter to Guinness's Assistant Managing Director C. K. Mill. It could not have been comforting for Guinness to receive this as the first communication from the new union claiming to represent its workers. Larkin was appalled by how the plebiscite had been conducted, most particularly with the use of the Guinness company letterhead and even with a record of each workers' name on his vote. Larkin reminded Guinness that they had, in their April 1948 notice to employees after the Labour Court decision, stated they acknowledged the right of every employee to join a trade union – a right that gave: 'freedom from coercion, intimidation or pressure, real or implied'.

The last paragraph of Larkin's two-page letter to Mill is a wonderful piece of writing turning the foremen's move back on its head:

> Clearly in the circumstances I have set out above, with reference to the circulation of these forms, it is not unnatural for employees to form the impression that pressure is being exercised upon them either officially or otherwise, and it is because my Union is satisfied it would not be the intention of your Board to seek to take away or invalidate the exercise of a right which they have publicly conceded and recognised that I have thought it right to bring this whole

matter to your urgent attention, and respectfully submit that the circulation of these forms should receive your immediate consideration, and that steps be taken to clarify a position which has placed your Board in a most invidious position and which, if it became publicly known, must create misunderstanding among the public, and resentment among the general body of trade unionists in this country.

One paragraph, one sentence and one message imbued with shades of Big Jim's 'tainted goods' method of industrial action. Mill immediately wrote back a brief and polite letter to Larkin assuring him that the company stood by its April 1948 assertion, stating: 'We are aware that certain deliberations on the subject are going on amongst our employees and that in connection therewith some kind of plebiscite has been organised. We regard this as a matter for the employees themselves and the company have not interfered in any way.'

Sir Charles Harvey was keeping Sir Hugh Beaver informed of developments (he described Larkin's letter as 'an outburst from Larkin accusing the Board of partiality'). He informed Beaver that the WUI was affiliated to the ITUC: 'This is considered more left than the Congress of Irish Unions'. Harvey had asked Morrissey in the Registry Department to write up information about the two main unions contending for the privilege of representing Guinness non-trade staff: the WUI and the ITGWU. Morrissey gave a financial and membership profile of both unions – ITGWU with a bank balance of £300,000 compared with the WUI's £13,500. ITGWU's membership total of 78,380 compared with the WUI's 13,225. Morrissey also gave a very competent history of the trade union movement in Ireland – though he wrongly stated that Jim Larkin had spent some years in Russia in the 1920s. He also noted: 'Larkin (Jr) spent some years in Russia, and appears to have similar ideas to his father on Trade Union activities'. This would have been frightening stuff to the gentlemen on the Guinness Board.

Harvey, in a cover note to Beaver when sending him the summary commented: 'I send herewith a very interesting note by Morrissey on the two main Unions in this country. It is sad that our men all appear to be joining the wrong one.'

Indeed, a very simple Guinness office memo summed up the sentiment: 'The Association of Brewery Employees dissolved, the more extreme members joining the Workers' Union of Ireland and the moderates forming the Guinness Employees Organisation. See separate files for each.'

But the Association was not dead yet and in the swirl of activity in the weeks following the fateful Mansion House general meeting there was another plot twist in the offing. Harvey reported in an office memorandum dated 17 June 1949 to Beaver and other top management that a man named Vincent Savino, honorary treasury of the Association, had approached his department head Mr Mortier on the day before the plebiscite: 'At this interview Savino had told Mr Mortier that he was certain he could persuade over 50% of the Executive Committee of the A. B. E., including the Chairman, Kiersey, to stop the whole business of joining a Union if the Board would give wider recognition to the Association.'

But the horse had already bolted, the plebiscite had been held, the GEO had formed and the WUI's Larkin was on the attack.

The Guinness Employees' Organisation was a clone of the Association and would soon be going down its predecessor's worn paths of trying to gain recognition from the Board. Set up by some foremen – a rank that had been against the Association – and by traditionalist non-trade workers, it was doomed to repeat the Association's futile attempts and ultimate failure.

Larkin, meanwhile, issued a new circular to the Guinness employees entitled 'Think Over This!' He summed up the history of the frustrations of the Association of Brewery Employees and pointed out the company's stated wish to deal with a recognised trade union. Shifting some figures around, he said that the plebiscite had only brought a decision by a third of the staff to vote against joining an outside union. 'It is now suggested the Board is prepared to negotiate on wages or conditions with the Works Committee,' he wrote. 'WHY? Why? What factor has intervened causing such a change in policy? THE WORKERS' UNION OF IRELAND!!!' Guinness management had shot itself in the foot. By resisting any change they had evoked the most extreme change. It is likely that if they had accepted the Association they would have allowed the forming of yet another cosy element to rub shoulders in the workers' Utopia that was the Guinness Brewery. Now Guinness management had to find their way through dealing with a radical union. Harvey wrote in an office memorandum: 'It remains to be seen how many men will in the end join the Union, but it is probable that a few are too far committed now to back out'.

'Big Jim' Larkin had once said that he did not just want bread on the table for every working family but a vase of flowers, too. When 'Young Jim' made his foothold for non-trade workers in Guinness he set out not only to give them a voice but to give them a vision. This, above all, is what won over Jack Carruthers and led him to devote himself to the WUI. Carruthers was highly respected by his fellow workers in the Cooperage Department and Jack Harte, wanting to promote the establishing of the WUI in the Brewery, went to Carruthers and asked him to attend an upcoming general meeting where Larkin would outline his plans for the union. Carruthers agreed to do so. Standing at the back of the hall, listening to Larkin, Carruthers was finally convinced that this would be the way forward and that something like the Guinness Employees' Organisation was futile. It was his turning point in this movement. He joined in the Union's recruiting drive, using all his considerable influence among his comrades, and would become one of the first shop stewards in the Cooperage Department.

Because the Union had not yet been officially recognised by the Brewery, however, it could not yet have shop stewards. Jack Harte was one of the first 'card collectors' – collecting union dues from the men for the WUI as the membership grew. Others joining in the growing movement to organise the men were people such as Joe O'Brien, Tommy Logan, Tommy Coleman and 'Doc' Hannigan. Paddy Cardiff, a worker in Guinness who would later become one of the leading lights of the Irish Labour movement, had been one of the first to join the WUI and recalled that in those early days there was a major recruiting drive among the men. Like Harte, Cardiff was an ex-British Army man. 'I had a certain amount of influence with the British ex-soldiers,' Cardiff recalled, 'and an awful lot of these flocked to the banner.' Cardiff believed that Carruthers, as an ex-soldier of the Irish army, was using his influence with that group of men. Recruiting men to the WUI was absolutely crucial: the higher the membership, the less scope there was for management to ignore the Union.

Jack Harte recalled that Mick Kiersey devoted himself more and more to recruiting new Guinness members to the WUI. He would stand outside the gates at the end of his working day and approach the men – the expression was 'breasting' – to encourage them. Someone made a complaint about this activity and the police arrived to move Kiersey away. He refused to be moved, stating he was on public, not private, property and was simply talking with his workmates. He could not be prevented from continuing his recruiting efforts.

At the start of September Larkin made the inevitable next move: he informed Sir Charles Harvey that he was seeking a pay increase of one pound a week for his members. Harvey wrote back asking how many of the Brewery staff the WUI represented. This was a move that had, when Guinness were dealing with the Association, stalled any chance of negotiations for months until a list of the employees was supplied and checked. When reporting to Beaver about having made this move Harvey wrote: 'If their reply shows that only a comparatively small number of our men have joined, we propose to tell them that in the circumstances we are not prepared to receive a deputation to discuss an increase of the basic wage'. But now the Brewery was dealing with Larkin who replied: 'I submitted your letter of the 8th instant to the General Executive Committee, and I am now instructed to indicate our surprise should you infer a responsible trade union would serve a claim on your firm without the prior authorisation of a sufficiently representative number of the employees concerned. Actually your request is unprecedented in our experience.' A rap on the knuckles for Sir Charles.

The Company had said that they wanted to deal with a professional trade union from outside the Brewery. They were now getting a taste of what that actually meant. Guinness stated that they would not meet representatives of the WUI until they had been shown the extent of union membership in the Brewery. The WUI simply did not respond.

The WUI campaign in the Guinness brewery gained pace. An eight-page document, under the front page banner 'The Gate Post', was issued as 'an organ of the Guinness Branch of the Workers' Union of Ireland' and it set out the full WUI case for recognition. It was stated that the document was the work of 'five Brewery employees who have had no previous experience in journalism', yet the influence of Larkin Jr was clear, given such quotes as this:

> Forty years and more ago the struggle was hard and bitter. Workers had to be aroused to their own degradation and slavelike conditions by agitation and appeals to their manhood. Little could be gained from the employers by argument or reason – only by industrial struggle, by the power and force of strike action. Every small increase in wages, reduction in hours, or other improvement in conditions had to be forced out of employers, and the workers had to fight even for the right to be members of a trade union at all. Those days are largely gone thanks to the organised action of trade unionists. Today your right to join a trade union is guaranteed by the Constitution of Ireland. Exercise that right now!

The pamphlet, produced by such brewery workers as Luke Shields, Vincent Savino, Paddy Bergin, Paddy Whelan and 'Doc' Hannigan, emphasised the difference between the Works Committee, at which matters could be 'discussed' and trade union representation where matters could be 'negotiated'. The Guinness Employees' Organisation was also dismissed: 'Have these people short memories, or do they prefer not to remember the facts. Further, do they not recall that at a recent Works Committee meeting, the Board re-stated their attitude in reply to a question about this organisation. They said that the GEO or any other internal organisation could not be recognised by them under any circumstances. Most men will agree that the ABE, which had a membership of 1,725, deserved much more respect than it received from the Board of Directors. Do the GEO with a much less representative membership expect or deserve any better?'

The pamphlet then turned its focus on the Works Committee, listing futile attempts at change through that system of such issues as pensions, grading system and shift work. It then quoted from the Chairman of the Works Committee: he said that 'the subjects so far raised were unsuitable and that they should give greater attention to matters concerning efficiency and discipline. He had further stated that they, as members of the Works Committee, had an obligation to the Board to use their influence to enforce greater discipline among the men.'

Having demonstrated the ineffectiveness of the Organisation and the Works Committee and in turn listed the strengths of the WUI (and throwing in a religious poem and a Papal quote in favour of trade unionism for good measure along the way), the pamphlet ended with:

> We hope that this bulletin has been of some value in promoting the case of trade unionism in the Brewery. It was realised by us that some such organ was necessary in order to keep our members up to date with events and further, to counter the slanderous propaganda which is being spread in the Brewery about our Union. These latter tactics are in keeping with the people concerned and we have nothing but the utmost contempt for them.
>
> Our consciences are clear, we have taken our stand for trade unionism and we have no apologies to offer: far too long have we fattened on the gains of other trade unionists; far too long have we let others fight our battles. Thank God we have shown that there is a little spirit left among the working-men of Guinness's.

At this time Harvey, however, was considering the possibility of recognising both the WUI and the new GEO but he first wanted to see how the restructuring of the Works Committee, with its new sub-committees, functioned. He instructed Buttanshaw to ask the GEO to wait a few months before a decision was made on their status in the Brewery.

By mid-October Larkin wrote to Harvey informing him that the WUI represented approximately 1,000 men in the Brewery but also saying that a problem had arisen for the union's members in the Malthouse and a meeting with management was urgently needed to discuss that and the pay increase. Harvey replied offering a date for a meeting between union and management (the head of the Labour Committee and the manager of the Registry department). It would be the first face-to-face meeting between the WUI and Guinness management.

The meeting took place at 2.30 PM on 31 October 1949 in the Manager's Office of the Registry Department. Buttanshaw and Morrissey, on the Guinness side, met Larkin, Ferguson and the Guinness WUI men Kiersey (now Chairman of the WUI branch), McGregor and Bergin. The latter was from the Malting Department and had come to state the situation about work conditions in that section.

Larkin proved his grounds for the pay increase with facts and figures – showing that Guinness had not raised wages to match the rise in cost of living since 1939 (average wages in Ireland had gone up by a third since 1939 whereas the cost of living had gone up by double that). He also showed how Guinness, traditionally the best-paying employer in Ireland, was now slipping behind other companies. For its part, the Guinness management could refer to a general agreement that had been established between the Labour Court, employers and trade unions for what was in effect a national pay agreement. They did not want to start 'a new bout of wage increases' by giving their labourers a raise. The discussion on that matter ended when Buttanshaw said the Board would write to the union about the issue.

There were two problems in the Malthouse. The first was that there were times when a task was given that took more time than expected and the men wound up doing unpaid overtime. The second was that the men, in tough working conditions, had nowhere to store or dry their clothes. On the first, a compromise was agreed for reviewing overtime in the department. On the second, Buttanshaw said that work was already under way to remedy the problem and the only delay was the post-war scarcity of materials.

Ferguson also asked for clarification on the procedure for how the men could deal with questions or complaints. Buttanshaw said the men should approach their Head of Department directly or through the Works Committee. If this did not lead to a satisfactory solution the men could go to the Union who could then write directly to the company.

The meeting lasted an hour. When Harvey wrote a memo to Beaver about the event, he added: 'C. K. M. (managing director Dr Charles King Mill) and I had a talk with Larkin afterward and he was on his best behaviour, assuring us that he had no intention of trying to force any employees who did not wish to join his Union into doing so.'

Harvey and Larkin had met. It was a brave and interesting move on Harvey's part to make this informal approach. Larkin was indeed inside St James's Gate, now shaking hands and chatting with some of the 'gods' of the Brewery. One can only imagine the first impressions when Harvey and Larkin met – the military man a shade taller than Larkin's towering father, the militant who was also a respected politician and intellectual – but they were heading into a long and complex journey together.

Entering into the unknown waters of a relationship with its non-tradesmen through a trade union, the Guinness company sought advice from the Federated Union of Employers about how to respond to the WUI. Guinness would soon join that Federation as part of its evolution into the changing world of industrial relations.

In tandem with this, the Guinness Employees' Organisation (sometimes also, confusingly, called the Organisation of Brewery Employees) was making its own moves in its attempts to counter the drift of workers towards the WUI. What they needed, they informed management, was some clear achievement they could show the men so as to convince them that they were recognised by management. They made a specific proposal: general ('tariff') workers had to have five years' service before receiving the full rate, even though they were doing the same work as men earning more than them. The full rate should be applied after a year's service. A man named Kinane, the honorary secretary of the Organisation, wrote: 'This is certainly the one tonic the men need to make them realise that an Outside Union is not the remedy for their ills.'

All of this was creating a chaotic structure of communication in the Brewery: management had already said, when rejecting the Association, that it recognised the right of the men to join a trade union. Then the Works Committee system had been set up – and extended to a sub-committee structure to improve worker-management lines of communication. Then the WUI was being acknowledged. Would the Organisation also be recognised? Within a matter of months the Brewery had gone from a tradition of management never dealing directly with the workers to a situation where there were a string of overlapping means for dealing with grievances. The question became: which line of communication would the workers choose? The management wanted the Works Committee system, already in operation at Park Royal, to be the choice. The foremen-led Organisation wanted the in-house system to be the choice. Larkin's men wanted the WUI to be the voice of the Guinness workers. The ITGWU had, by now, faded away from the Brewery.

But there was only one issue for negotiation that would convince the non-tradesmen in the Brewery: a wage increase. Guinness had only ever set its own rates of pay for the non-trade workers – wages for tradesmen were established by their unions and were the same throughout the country. The Association had tried and failed to get a wage increase for its members. Larkin had presented his case for a wage increase but in November Harvey, having consulted with other brewery employers such as Beamish and Crawford as well as the Federated Union of Employers, wrote to Larkin stating the old line: 'Our Board constantly and regularly keeps in review the trend of wage levels as related to the circumstances existing from time to time, and we are satisfied that at present our scale of wages conforms to these levels.'

It was time for the Workers' Union of Ireland to get in the ring with Guinness in the battle for more pay. Larkin had already decided to wind down his political commitments, resigning as leader of the Labour Party in November 1949 to focus more energy on his trade union work. Days after his resignation Larkin wrote to Harvey. There was a national agreement in effect between the Irish Trade Union Congress and the Federated Union of Employers, as overseen by the Labour Court. But Larkin presented statistics showing that wage increases in the Brewery had not kept pace with the rise in profits: between 1938 and 1947 Guinness profits had grown by 96 percent, its prices had risen 99 percent but wages had only increased 76 percent. These 'anomalous circumstances' were Larkin's ground for seeking a pay increase for the workers he represented and he was taking his case to the Labour Court. He planned, at the same time, to raise with the Court the matter of the 'conciliation machinery' in the Brewery. With regard to this latter point, Harvey wrote to Larkin: 'the existing machinery gives full facilities for ventilating all such questions, and if there are any grievances in this connection I suggest they are a matter for discussion by the Works Committee and Departmental Sub-Committees'. The focus for Harvey and the Guinness management would be on fighting off the wage increase bid.

This was the first real test of the two sides. Two years after the Association had faced Guinness at the Labour Court, the WUI were now taking up the torch on behalf of the workers.

Preparations for the battle were intense. While the Association had presented a case for a wage increase that was vague and emotive, Larkin and his men put together a meticulous case that piled fact upon fact: quotes on profits and company dividends as compared with rates of pay. On the Guinness side there was a frenzy of number crunching when Harvey ordered that the Larkin statistics be investigated. Harvey also informed Larkin that the Works Committee and departmental sub-committees worked perfectly fine as instruments for conciliation, so there was no grounds for change on that front.

The Guinness senior accountant came back to Harvey with an analysis of the figures and showed that Larkin's statistics were not correct. The rise in profits and prices – the latter largely caused by increased excise duties – were not as high as Larkin claimed. Also, increased manufacturing costs had not been included in Larkin's figures. The accountant could demonstrate that Guinness labourers earned on average 9 percent more than other labourers.

Larkin, meanwhile, published another 'Gate Post' for the Guinness workers and some of its claims were angering Harvey who wrote a memorandum to heads of departments about its content. The newsletter made such accusations as: 'a man's record is kept on a secret file (a la OGPU).' This was a great provocation from Moscow-educated leftist Larkin – the OGPU was the forerunner of the KGB in the totalitarian Soviet Union.

The Gate Post issue also accused: 'The present facilities for washing and dressing are primitive and degrading and all that we get are vague promises for the future' and 'in certain departments the Conditions of Employment Acts are blatantly flouted'. Harvey demanded: 'Will the Manager, Registry Department, obtain confirmation from each department that this accusation is untrue'.

In the lead up to the Labour Court hearing, Harvey asked Morrissey to clarify with the WUI what it would be seeking. Ferguson reiterated the wage claim of an increase of one pound per week. With regard to the negotiating machinery he set out three levels of communication:

> 1) Individual cases at Foreman/Shop Steward level in the first instance.
> 2) Matters of more general interest affecting a number of men in a department at Branch Committee/Departmental Head level in the first instance.
> 3) Union/Management level.

This was the union model of communication. It would take years before Guinness management woke up to it. Larkin and Ferguson requested a meeting with Harvey to discuss this process but he declined. Within days of this an official notice was posted in the Brewery reiterating the Brewery's system of dealing with grievances.

The Labour Court hearing was held on Tuesday 14 March 1950. This was right in the middle of another, well-publicised, case that the WUI had brought to the Labour Court seeking the right to represent workers in the Hospital Trust, Ltd (the company that ran the Irish Hospital Sweepstakes). The Trust had, according to Ferguson when presenting the WUI case in the Court, fought against the workers who had joined the union: 'The supervisors immediately began a campaign of intimidation, talking of Communist intrigues, threatening victimisation and so on. Copies of the Bishop of Galway's Lenten Pastoral were pinned on the doors, passages underlined, and the message distorted. Unsigned leaflets were openly passed around, with the obvious approval of supervisors, slandering the Union and its leading officers.' In the end, the Labour Court instructed the Trust that the WUI had the right to represent the Company's workers. But the case was a good example of the climate created once the WUI showed up at a company's door.

Guinness came to the Labour Court armed with an artillery of statistics showing that they were keeping pace with wage increases and were not making extra profits. They listed all the pay increases they had given their 2,381 non-tradesmen since the end of the Standstill Order and demonstrated that they had adhered to the terms of the national agreement that had been established: and meanwhile their shareholders had not had an increase in dividend since 1933. It was a thorough and strong case, topped off by saying that if they gave a pay increase it might start another round of rising costs and pay claims throughout the economy. They went on to list the many improvements in working conditions being undertaken now that the hardships of wartime had ended: an impressive programme of better facilities; a plan for building houses in Terenure for the families of 236 Guinness workers at a cost of half a million pounds; continuing to provide low-rate building society loans for the workers. On top of this the company had changed its Pension Fund from being 'at the pleasure of the Board' to being contractual, with almost two million pounds transferred from the company to Trustees and a promise of a further two-and-a-half million pounds in the coming years.

Guinness really was a great employer and their presentation at the Labour Court set out just how generous and forward-thinking they were.

Turning to the matter of the conciliation process, Harvey pointed out that there were still more non-trade unionists than trade unionists among the labourers and that the Works Committee could serve both alike while the WUI could not. The option of a trade union member taking a grievance to management through his union was always available, whereas the Works Committee was the only system that would be available to an employee who did not want to join a trade union. Here, Harvey displayed the disconnect between worker and boss that he was unaware of: 'Any man wishing to make a request or complaint may ask his Fore-man to arrange a personal interview for him with the Head of his Department. If he so desires he may be accompanied by or have his case put for him by his departmental representative on the Central Works Committee. If then he is not satisfied, he has the right to appeal in writing to the Board'. When Larkin came around to that subject, he would pull the ground out from under Harvey's feet. Guinness had made a strategic mistake: they had focused all their energy on rejecting the pay increase without realising that their real Achilles heel was how they communicated with their workers.

Larkin's case with regard to the pay increase followed a different line of approach: not how much the Guinness labourers earned compared with other labourers but how much they earned compared with the scale of Guinness profits. It was a pure leftist argument. He acknowledged the value of the pension scheme but pointed out that: 'While waiting for the years to pass in order to receive a pension a worker must maintain himself and his family and a good pension scheme, no matter how much appreciated, will not ease the workers' present living difficulties from week to week. In fact it is well known that workers must perforce live from week to week, leaving the years to come to kindly providence.'

Larkin's view was that the high profits Guinness enjoyed, as opposed to the minutiae of whether the pay rises had kept pace with cost of living, should guide their rates of pay. He stated: 'Can the Court picture a situation in which a firm could concede our full claim of one pound per week increase in wages and at the expense of only 5% of the 1948/49 net profit, which amounted to £2,073,000?' He demonstrated that the basic labourer wage in Guinness's, at five pounds eleven shillings for a five-and-a-half day forty-four hour week, was only middle of the range for a Dublin labourer whereas, before the war, Guinness workers were the highest paid. Interestingly, Larkin also made several references to how wrong it would be for Guinness to 'completely' or 'wholly' reject the claim for a wage increase. He was perhaps hinting that if the Union came away from the Court with some form of increase he would be satisfied.

As for the matter of shareholder dividends, Larkin could quote facts and figures demonstrating that over the previous fourteen years, thirty-one million pounds had been paid out in dividends – one and a quarter million pounds in the 1948/49 fiscal year. Again driving home the small cost of the increase he compared it with the dividends: 'the cost of conceding our claim would amount to £104,000 for a year'.

Larkin then moved on to the matter of the conciliation process in the Brewery. Here, he quoted back to Guinness their own statement, when it had been to the Labour Court with the Association, that it could not agree to allow the Association to usurp the functions of an official trade union. Larkin detailed the structure and severe limitations of the Works Committee set up by Harvey and explained how the Association had given this a trial: 'This body which deals with matters of importance to Brewery employees as a whole meets every two months for ninety minutes. Decisions are announced at the next meeting two months afterwards. Is it any wonder the employees feel the Works Committee is nothing more than a smoke screen thrown out by the Board in an endeavour to cover up the absence of any effective machinery whatever.'

He dismissed the Guinness notion of being in touch with its labourers' needs: 'If the employers in this case were the model people they are popularly supposed to be, anticipating sympathetically every need of their workers then perhaps this extraordinary state of affairs might be understood. But in the two applications before you today, gentlemen, it is abundantly clear no matter who may believe Guinness's is a sort of Glocamorra the employees emphatically do not'.

Larkin then turned, with venom, on the fines system the company had set up in 1910 based on the 1896 Trucks Act: 'We have had many political changes in this country since 1896, but so far as Messrs Guinness go the British Truck Act is still a perfectly good Act and the authority conferred on the Company is exercised to the limit'. The Act gave supervisors the authority to dock fines ranging from a shilling to thirty shillings from labourers' wages for real or alleged misdemeanours. Larkin listed examples; a man fined a pound when caught smoking by the brewery police, a man fined one pound for declining overtime he was instructed to do at short notice because he had an important family engagement, a man with thirty years service was reduced in pay grade for being caught smoking: this was his only 'offence' in all his years of service, a man called in on emergency duty at 3 PM on Christmas Day and still working the following 6 AM was told he had stayed on deliberately to make extra money and was paid basic rate only. The incident was then entered in his record as a crime.

It would be interesting to know if Harvey, sitting in the Court, was hearing about such things for the first time. It is more than likely so. It was surely a shock for him, not least given his military background, to learn of such treatment of the lower-echelon troops in the company he managed. It was most certainly not in his nature to condone something like that.

Larkin explained that a man could appeal against a fine: the only way of doing so being to go to the department head who had fined him and submit the appeal through him to the Board. Larkin stated: 'We know of only one case of this kind and he was ultimately informed the Board had full confidence in the Department

Head.' Larkin pointed out that even when the management revised the powers and structure of the Works Committee an employee with a grievance could still only pursue it through his supervisor, with or without a Committee representative who would be a fellow-employee and therefore not capable of being neutral in the case. He concluded: 'We submit a proper system of negotiation for resolving problems individual and collective at all levels is in a sense of much greater importance to the Board even than it is to the men. Clearly if a residue of discontent, arising from sheer frustration, is to remain after every complaint then one day in the very near future we shall inevitably reach a state of things utterly unreasonable and from which it will not be easy to escape'.

Two weeks later, the Labour Court gave its judgement. It ruled against a wage increase, seeing no reason why Guinness labourers should, as a matter of course or precedent, earn more than other labourers. Their rate was on par with that of other men. The Court also agreed with the Guinness view that if their men received a pay increase this might trigger wage claims in other companies.

On the matter of dealing with grievances, however, the Court largely supported the union. They said of the Works Committee: 'It does not seem to the Court that the present machinery is entirely satisfactory, especially as the staff side of the Works Committee includes representatives of tradesmen and foremen who would not be directly interested in the conditions of service of labourers'. This was, of course, the greatest flaw of the Works Committee, even though Harvey would not yet concede to that fact. The Court stated that an employee was free to involve his shop steward in any approach to a department head: 'The Court recommends that a labourer should be allowed, if he so desires, to invoke the assistance of the Union shop steward in his Department or of any other worker in the Department when applying to his Departmental head, and that if the matter is not settled at that stage a Union member should be allowed to be represented by a Branch or Head Office official of the Union at any later stage of the discussion'. That was a key statement. In a somewhat convoluted ruling, the Court said that wages and conditions could not be the sole province of the trade union but rather would be discussed by sub-committees – and that a union official could be invited on to the sub-committee. The ruling also said: 'If the Union is not satisfied with the result of the discussions in the sub-committee, it should be entitled to direct consultation with the management.'

Harvey telegraphed a message to Beaver about the outcome, informing him that the wage claim had been rejected and that the Court had 'made some minor recommendations regarding our negotiating machinery'. Beaver replied: 'Thank you very much for your very charming note'. It was a surprisingly naïve exchange between two such intelligent people. Both men were underestimating Larkin if they thought the Court ruling had done to him what it had done to the Association. Larkin's union had been accepted as part of the Guinness negotiation process. He was officially, with Labour Court approval, inside the gates. He would now use that ruling as leverage to build the power and influence of his union in the Brewery. The real changes had only just begun.

Five

The Rise

A general meeting of WUI Guinness employees was held at the Mansion House on 3 April 1950 at which the findings of the Labour Court were presented. Larkin declared, perhaps with an intended pun: 'The rejection by the Labour Court of the claim of Guinness's workers for improved wage rates must leave a bad taste in the mouth of every thoughtful person, whether he be an ordinary trade union member or official, any interested member of the public or believer in any principles or system of social justice.' He also pointed out the injustice of a situation where, he said, 'The Labour Court has now officially declared that it is quite fair and proper that a worker be required to produce forty shillings in profits for his employers for every twenty shillings he produces in wages for himself and his family, and not satisfied with this Victorian economic dictum blindly refuses to even inquire as to what standard of life the worker can maintain on such wages.'

The meeting voted unanimously against the wage increase refusal and unanimously for the change in the grievance system. While that would hardly have come as a surprise to Guinness management, a development later in the month would have been cause for concern: the Irish Trade Union Congress decided to give the Labour Court a contractual three-month notice that it was quitting the national wage agreement. Larkin's union was part of the ITUC and a line of his argument in the Labour Court – that the working population had a low standard of living while providing substantial increases in production and profits – was the ITUC's grounds for leaving the agreement.

Ireland at this time was being ruled by what was known as 'the first inter-party government' – a rainbow coalition that managed to oust Fianna Fáil from office for the first time in sixteen years. Seán Lemass had served as Minister for Industry and Commerce for most of those years and attacked the new government in the Dáil for letting the standard of living for the working population slide. He stated that in real terms workers were 7 percent worse off than they had been before the war. Pressure was growing on all sides for a raise in wages.

Larkin contacted Harvey for a meeting and Harvey agreed. Knowing full well what Larkin still sought, Harvey prepared for the meeting: the senior accountant of the Brewery did a thorough examination of issues related to company profit versus pay rates. The average wage earner received £405 a year (this is a figure reached by including all levels of employees in the Brewery) while the company made an average of £900 a year profit per employee. The workers were 7 percent more productive in 1949 than they had been in 1938, but the report added: 'Is the Union prepared to concede that if production falls this is due to 'lessened effort' on the part of the workers who should in that case accept reduction in wages?' Morrissey warned, ahead of the meeting: 'It would appear undesirable for the Company to have conferences with the Workers' Union of Ireland in the hope that some new formula acceptable to the Union would emerge, as any agreement made by us would be used by the Union as a spearhead in its claims on other employers, or in the consideration of a new agreed general wages formula.' A week ahead of the meeting Harvey issued an office memorandum laying out his planned strategy for the meeting: 'I will do my best to avoid discussing any details, but if Larkin insists on discussing the question of profits vis a vis wages I shall point out to him that it might well be argued that if there are any profits to spare after we have paid for the very large reconstruction programme to which we are committed, our first duty is towards the shareholders whose money it is which has financed the business. These shareholders have received no increase at all since 1939, whereas the wage earners have gone up by over 70%.'

Larkin and Ferguson faced Harvey and Morrissey on 10 July 1950. Larkin announced that the WUI now represented 1,300 Guinness workers and that the number would increase if the Brewery fully accepted the union: which could represent the men better than a Works Committee or House Association. Harvey said he could not accept the union as speaking for all men – and that there were many who did not want to join a union. Interestingly, Harvey added that 'from some points of view it might be preferable to have to deal with the Union only, but the facts being as they were he could not do so'. Larkin submitted, as expected, that some form of wage increase was due – be it even in areas of allowances on differential payments. Harvey said that there would be no move on wages until the national situation became clear – the national agreement would expire at the end of August. The third and final item on the agenda of the meeting was the 'conciliation machinery'. This had been the one clear in-road established by the Labour Court ruling but again there was no budge on Harvey's side: matters would be dealt with primarily 'in-house' and the trade union would be called on only if that process was failing for an individual or issue.

Harvey was still holding a conservative line: before the meeting ended, he announced that while he would be generally prepared to meet Larkin and Ferguson he would rather they did not bring with them a representative of the Brewery workers unless it was absolutely necessary for some specific reason. He felt that 'men of the Nos. 2 or 3 Grades or below should not have the right of access to the Board over the heads of No. 1 Grade Foremen.' Harvey felt it was up to him to maintain the status of the foremen. Ferguson, certainly taken aback by this, said it would be very difficult to agree with that as it was against the normal rules of trade union procedure. Both sides agreed that they had expressed their views and did not have to make a definite decision as yet. The meeting, 'which had been conducted throughout in a friendly atmosphere', ended. Larkin walked away from it with little if any progress. Harvey had held the traditional Guinness ground.

The Irish Trade Union Congress had its annual meeting in Galway later the same month and the theme of increased profits combined with increased Irish worker productivity led the way: 'Workers require an increase in wages, workers have earned it and it can be conceded out of profits,' the *Evening Mail* quoted ITUC president Sam Kyle as saying. The *Irish Times* reported Larkin in much more forthright form: 'We will not be satisfied with just a share of the national cake. We are going to have the biggest share. We are going forward and upward, and there is no limit to our demands.'

The Federated Union of Employers, which the Guinness company joined in 1950, were being approached by the split trade union congresses – the ITUC and the CIU – with their reasons for a national wage increase but the employers were unconvinced and decided to submit their views to the Labour Court. The report on the FUE's congress to debate wage increases concluded with the Chairman's view: 'The unions would now no doubt press forward with individual claims, but this would at least be a slower process, and he believed that if employers stood firm few Unions would be in a financial position to support unreasonable demands. He hoped that any employer who received a claim would at once notify others who were likely to be concerned. This would prevent a situation developing in which some employers might agree to the demands made on them because they were not aware of the general trend of Union claims.' It was the terrible weakness triggered by the split between 'Big Jim' Larkin and O'Brien, and it was a great source of frustration to James Larkin to see this as part of his father's legacy.

Meanwhile back in the Brewery there had been a tiny victory for the Union on the factory floor. A union member in the small Offices Department had a grievance but had no shop steward in the department to represent him. Morrissey of the Registry Department had not allowed him to bring in Mick McGregor, Branch Secretary and also a shop steward in the Brewhouse Department, to discuss the matter with the man's department head, stating: 'as McGregor was not employed in the Offices Department he could not therefore represent or accompany Reid in applying to the Head of the Offices Department'. Larkin and Ferguson objected to this and Morrissey, at Larkin's request, reported the matter – and the stance he was taking – to Harvey. Morrissey had behaved in accordance with what he understood to be agreed from the Labour Court decision. Harvey wrote to the WUI about the matter, requesting also a list of shop stewards which was then provided to him. The word came down from Harvey that in a case where a union man did not have a shop steward in his own department he could bring one in from elsewhere. It was some small mark of respect for the union. The list provided was of forty shop stewards established in the Brewery, among them J. V. Harte in the Brewhouse.

There was another victory: as union membership grew, Charlie Evenden became the first brewery policeman to join the WUI. Evenden was a very popular figure and had been a prize-winning welter-weight boxer, so his joining was a big morale-booster for those promoting union membership. He would eventually become shop steward for the Brewery Police when they, after several years, decided to join the WUI.

While moves were being made for a pay increase on the national level, the WUI shifted its attention to specific issues in the Guinness brewery. The correspondence now came from Ferguson rather than Larkin, who was probably too busy with his political duties as TD to engage in specific WUI duties. The union took on the cases of individuals and departments with grievances. It outlined hardships for workers in the kieves (where Jack Harte was a shop steward): 'The scales that form on the copper come away in a powdery form, the men willy-nilly inhaling it leaving a residue in throats and mouths that fouls the taste of food and drink subsequently taken. Apart from this, they must contend with the intense heat caused by steam leaking through the coils and heaters. Indeed men would be severely burned were they to touch the latter with bare skin, and accidents of this kind have occurred'. The union also raised the issue of men in the boiler-house department who had lost grades and pay when shifted because of the staffing of a new power station. Harvey responded to the issues, but no major progress was made. Regarding the men in the boiler-house he wrote: 'you will appreciate that for a modern power station we require more than mere muscle, and some of the old stokers who were quite adequate for stoking a boiler were not suitable for the new Power Station'.

At the national level talks in the Labour Court between unions and employers broke down and Larkin was part of a deputation of union representatives meeting with the Taoiseach, ministers and other government representatives in November.

The Congress of Irish Unions – the alliance that had broken away along with O'Brien's ITGWU in the face of Larkin's WUI being allowed to join the Irish Trade Union Congress – instructed their unions to press for a twelve-shillings-per-week pay increase. The meetings back and forth between the two trade union congresses, the FUE and government, had not yielded a clear result and strikes were looming. As Christmas 1950 approached there was a likelihood that Dublin would be without a gas supply.

In early November the Taoiseach, John Costello, summoned a crisis meeting with the FUE at which the government sought a concerted effort from employers to bring down the cost of living and raise wages. The FUE responded that they had no mandate to carry out the former and were unconvinced of the need for the latter. Senator Maguire of the FUE expressed the view 'that the ordinary worker would be satisfied to be left alone, but leaders are adopting world socialistic methods of creating dissatisfaction. These leaders stated that employers were solely responsible for the high prices and that they alone could bring them down'.

The FUE were not giving ground, although plainly the government needed them to do so. Senator Douglas, with the FUE, stated that 'he felt the present position was a challenge to private enterprise and, possibly, to the State. There was no justification for agreeing with Labour to establish an all round increase, although, with his experience in politics, he did not pay much attention to the many statements made outside. He suggested that more publicity should be given to substantiate the Cost of Living figure'.

A week later, the FUE met again – Morrissey, manager of the Registry Department, attended on behalf of Guinness – to report back on that government meeting and another follow-up meeting. The main block between union and employers was the cause of the rising cost of living: were wage increases simply creating an endless spiral. Yet the employers were fully aware of the problem the unions were trying to correct. Morrissey's account of the meeting states: 'Mr Kellett, Draper, mentioned that the 7/6d increase which the Drapers agreed to grant to their van drivers and packers was made up of 2/6d to bring their wage increase to 81% of the 1939 wage, and the other 5/- in anticipation of an increase in the cost-of-living index.' So the claims being made by the unions were true. Realising what they were admitting, it was agreed among this group of employers that the outcome of their meeting would not be revealed to the press.

The WUI were passing out leaflets in the Brewery, signed by Ferguson, using this national pressure for a pay increase as part of their recruitment drive:

> Just consider what the level of wages and salaries would be had organised employees not forced the pace in the race to close the gap between wages and prices. Even in the brewery can any man deny his present rates are the result, and the direct consequence of wage increases brought about by trade union action outside.
>
> DID YOU GET YOUR LAST INCREASE BEFORE OR AFTER THE TRADE UNIONS HAD NEGOTIATED THE ELEVEN SHILLING FORMULA?
>
> Apart altogether from wage rates, there are important grievances relating to conditions of employment that need to be adjusted from time to time.
>
> In this work and in endless other ways the trade union provides skilled assistance, operated on a strictly impersonal basis and without fear of favour.
>
> BUT THE STRONGEST OF ALL APPEALS SHOULD BE BASED UPON THAT DIRECTED TO A WORKER'S SELF RESPECT. HAVE YOU EXPERIENCED THAT FEELING OF EXULTATION THAT COMES FROM POSSESSION OF THE UNION CARD, INDICATING YOU UPHOLD THE ONLY VALUE THAT MATTERS TO THE WORKERS ON THE JOB; 'AN INJURY TO ONE IS THE CONCERN OF ALL.'

Taking the natural next step, the WUI made its inevitable move: Ferguson wrote to the Brewery on 21 December outlining the union's case for a one pound per week pay increase for its members. The WUI was ready for a re-match with Guinness's. The case it presented was much the same as that which had failed before the Labour Court in March. Undaunted, the union also referred its claim to the Labour Court.

Guinness – whether or not they were influenced by pressure from the WUI – announced in January 1951 a set of 'temporary increases to meet present conditions' in wages as well as some individual changes in pay conditions for people on night shift etc. The increase was less than a quarter of what the WUI were seeking, but was ultimately accepted by the WUI in conjunction with an annual bonus paid out by the Brewery. In the months that followed there were further discussions and piecemeal increases – with companies like John Jameson whiskey and John Players tobacco reaching agreement with their non-trade workers and these companies keeping each other informed of developments and decisions.

But there was still a tug-of-war going on between Harvey and the WUI with regard to how matters were negotiated. Harvey sent out an office memo in January reporting on a 'conference' with heads of departments to discuss the role of shop stewards following the Labour Court ruling of the previous March. He wrote:

> It was agreed that non-tradesmen shop stewards could not be treated in the same way as shop stewards in the various trades where they represent 100% of the men, and it was most desirable in any way to undermine either the authority of the foremen or the effectiveness of the departmental sub-committees.
>
> It was agreed, therefore, that the functions of shop stewards representing non-tradesmen were two-fold only:-
>
> (a) representing individuals before the heads of departments if asked to do so by the individual;
>
> (b) reporting to the Trade Union if the men whom they represent were not satisfied with the results of any action which might have been taken by the departmental sub-committee or heads of department.

Harvey was certainly a man who knew how to stand his ground: he continued to believe that the two pillars of the communication process were the foremen and the Works Committees. This company line was soon put to the test, however. Ferguson had written to Harvey requesting a meeting to discuss wage-related matters: the abolition of 'service money' for Grade 5, and the growing discrepancy between pay rates for Grades 2, 3 and 4. Harvey responded that: 'As the points you have raised concern all employees, whether members of your Union or not, I think the correct procedure would be to discuss them at a sub-committee meeting of the Central Works Committee.'

Harvey was committed to using the communication system he had established in the Brewery and so instead of previous union/management discussions in which three or so people sat at either side of the table, Ferguson was the sole WUI representative at a meeting on Wednesday 14 March 1951 of twelve men representing the kaleidoscope of Guinness management and staff at this meeting of the 'Special sub-committee of the Works Committee'. Also present was a representative, Traynor, of the still-breathing Guinness Employee's Organisation and non-tradesman foreman Farnan, who had been part of the original delegation to management protesting against the establishing of the Association of Brewery Employees.

Harvey said he would only be present at the meeting as an observer: 'primarily in order that the members of the Committee, and Messrs Ferguson and Traynor, might be assured that the Board was fully informed of the views expressed at the meeting, and of the manner in which they were put forward'. Buttanshaw chaired the meeting – and from the minutes it would seem that all had their say from the point of view of their section. And that nothing was agreed. It was exactly the problem highlighted in the 'Gate Post' circular: in this setting, matters could be discussed but not negotiated. Ferguson, known as a man with a temper, was surely seething as he endured the process. He presented his case, Buttanshaw and Morrissey explained why his case wasn't valid, others chimed in, and that was that.

The meeting lasted eighty minutes and at its conclusion Harvey said he would discuss the proceedings with other members of the Board but thought the claims proposed at the meeting would not meet with success. Within a week he informed the Central Works Committee (with a copy to Ferguson) that the WUI proposals had been rejected.

Harvey had continued to hold the line: the Board, and the Board alone, decided wage increases for its employees. But, as events would show, something happened to Sir Charles Harvey as he sat quietly observing the Works Committee he had established and supported. Somehow he had a crucial change of mind either at that meeting or in his own reflections on the proceedings. It was a trade union epiphany.

In May, Harvey wrote to Sir Hugh Beaver expressing great concerns about the fact that rates of pay in the Brewery were falling behind those for general labourers in Dublin because wages in the city were 'rocketing'. Harvey wrote: 'We have come to the conclusion that it is necessary for us to revise our wages before we are forced to do so on account of agitation created by the Workers' Union of Ireland.' It was interesting that he wanted to stay one step ahead of the union – preferring to anticipate agitation from them in order to avoid wage negotiations with them. The round of wage increases proposed by Harvey put brewery workers back to their traditional place ahead of other Dublin workers. It also made the adjustments required to balance out the discrepancy Ferguson had pointed out between the lower grades. Beaver approved the changes and a notice was issued to brewery workers informing them of the Board's decision to raise their rates of pay. The WUI called a general meeting of its members to discuss the pay rise and Ferguson wrote afterward to Harvey saying that the increase should be back-dated to January. Harvey, after consulting with Buttanshaw, responded that this would not be possible. Guinness, the great benefactor, had made its decision and awarded its pay increase as it saw fit. There could be no change and no further discussion.

In the Report article written about Ferguson it was said of him: 'The key to successful trade union negotiations is to know what is possible, and how to make possibilities become realities – of course, a successful trade union negotiator must also be able to create his own "possibilities".' In July 1951 that's what Ferguson did when he wrote a long, frank letter to Harvey that turned out to be pivotal. He informed Harvey that the Brewery Branch Committee accepted, 'after an exhaustive discussion', that there would be no back-pay. But Ferguson had some union/management savvy to impart. He wrote:

> Arising out of the Committee's decision it became very clear that some alteration in the machinery of negotiation as between your Board and this trade union will need to be considered. Although we recognise freely that the two increases compare favourably with wage adjustments to similar categories outside, the manner in which they were given, by Court order as it were from which there is no appeal, continues to create psychological difficulties. The whole method is peculiar (to the brewery) and foreign to the spirit of negotiations proper as between employers and workers. To begin with, there is a rule of thumb method practised in negotiation, whereby it is generally felt by employees that the first offer of an employer, following an application for an increase, is usually less than the employer may ultimately be induced to concede, and thus almost invariably the first offer is rejected and the employees feel greater satisfaction with the second offer, feeling that this is the maximum to be achieved in the given circumstances. I, personally, do not, and I am sure neither does your good self, agree with this system of horse trading, nor is there any reason for it at all, yet nevertheless we must recognise as realists the practice has grown up, it is uncomplicated to workers, is easily understood, and carries with it the maximum psychological satisfaction.

It was an extraordinarily blunt lesson from an experienced trade union negotiator to a hugely experienced military man who had never fully settled into cosy Guinness corporate life. Ferguson was putting his cards on the table, saying in effect 'this is how to play the game'.

Ferguson told Harvey that the WUI membership in the Brewery had reached 1,800. He also pointed out in his letter that the Guinness Employees' Organisation had reached such a point of collapse that its own chairman had joined the WUI.

Ferguson stated that the union now wanted sole right to negotiate with the Brewery in matters of wages and conditions for the employees. He concluded:

> I wish to impress upon you and the Board in the most forcible possible manner that unless you are prepared to effect the change in method as indicated in the immediate future, it will not be possible for this trade union to continue to exercise discipline among your employees. In all good faith we are seeking your co-operation in an effort to abate the growing resentment and frustration that the present methods of negotiation are causing.

Harvey was being asked to abandon the company-defined method of employer/employee communication and let a trade union lead the way in this dialogue. It would be a major step – and Harvey accepted it almost without reserve. Something had happened, between the direct meetings of the WUI and management and his observing the sub-committee of the Works Committee in action, to change his perspective. Sir Charles Harvey was a realist. In the past he had been tried and tested in military life and on the battle field. As the situation in the Guinness brewery became more complicated and the Irish workforce in general became more restless he was exactly what the company needed: the right man in the right place at the right time. He acknowledged that the Works Committee and sub-committee systems established by him in the Brewery had not been effective. He was willing to change with the times. One dissenting voice came from Registry Department head Morrissey. He advised against giving the WUI the sole right as negotiators they were seeking. He warned of the unions 'Communist' leanings and how this might lead employees to discontinue membership in the future. Morrissey also reported that he had discussed the matter with John O'Brien, Chairman of the FUE, who was: 'strongly of the opinion that this request should not be acceded to, as it would mean agreeing with the "closed shop" policy, and so far as he knows no employer here has agreed to such a claim in the case of general workers. It is accepted, of course, in the case of skilled workers.'

A date of 27 August 1951 was set for Harvey and his men to meet Larkin and Ferguson to discuss the issue. They were back to sitting across a table from each other, negotiating. Since Larkin and Harvey last met, the country had gone through another premature general election and this time Fianna Fáil returned to power as a minority government. Larkin comfortably held his seat. The non-trade staff of Guinness was 2,527 men and 190 'lads and boys'. Harvey wanted to know exactly how many of these the union represented. Above all, though, Harvey wanted the union to agree to certain conditions: that while they would be the only union being dealt with in regard to non-trade employees the company reserved the right to hear representations from 'any man, group of men or house association'. The WUI had to promise that they would put no employee under pressure to join the union. The WUI also had to accept that joining a trade union would never be a condition of employment in the Brewery. That last point was one that would become a core issue for the WUI.

In notes prepared for the meeting, there is one very significant comment with regard the procedure for wage increases: 'Normally first approach will now come from the Union, and except as regard bonuses the Board will no longer exercise its paternal anticipation.' Guinness, instead of being the benign master, decided they would listen. It was an acknowledgment of a maturing management and workforce.

The meeting went well. The following day Harvey sent Ferguson a draft of the notice that would be posted by management in the Brewery outlining the new status of the WUI and the terms agreed. He wanted to know if the union required any changes to the draft – itself an extraordinary shift in thinking on behalf of the brewery management. And yet another concession was made: management agreed that the union could bring an employee representative to negotiation meetings with the Board. This was something Harvey had originally sought not to allow: a non-tradesman meeting a member of the Board. For its part, the union agreed that if they brought a non-trade employee to a Board meeting management had the right to bring a foreman. It was part of the management's continuing efforts to bolster the fading prestige of the foremen.

The notice, which the union and the Guinness branch committee supported without any request for alteration, was posted in the Brewery on 3 September 1951. It announced that the sub-committee management set up for discussing wages and working conditions following the shift of the Association over to the WUI had disbanded. It stated that the Board: 'agreed to negotiate with the Workers' Union of Ireland in the normal way on general questions of wages and conditions of service so long as the Union continues to represent a substantial majority'. The notice concluded: 'The Board trust that the pleasant relations which have always existed between the management and the employees will in no way be affected by these new arrangements and that all employees, whether members of a Union or not, will continue to work together in the same friendly spirit as they have always done in the past'.

From then on, six years after the struggles of the Association of Brewery Employees began among the non-tradesmen, Larkin's union was the voice of the non-trade workers in Guinness's.

There was a last gasp for the old ways. The Guinness Employees' Organisation met with Harvey, requesting that the old structure of sub-committees still be allowed to propose wage claims. Harvey told them that they could indeed do so – but the Board would take no action until consulting with the WUI. The GEO asked that one of their representatives be present at negotiations between management and union – Harvey declined this, also. The era of the in-house structure was over and the WUI had gained the coveted role as the chosen trade union for Guinness and its non-trade employees. Creighton, Chairman of the GEO, said in conclusion that he: 'doubted very much whether the WUI really had the substantial majority they claimed, and said that most of their so-called members paid the shilling a week just to escape trouble. Many of the members of the GEO were in this latter category'.

As per a request from Harvey, Ferguson supplied an updated list of the elected shop stewards in the Brewery: now numbering almost fifty. Harvey took the list provided and distributed it to the six department heads (Cooperage, Brewhouse, Engineers, Malthouse, Refreshment, Traffic) so that they knew who was authorised to deal with them. The non-tradesmen were ceasing to be numbers: the men representing them had actual names to be noted by department heads! These were shop stewards representing the kaleidoscope of jobs such as Shiving, Cleansing, Circuit Train, Scaffolders, Laggers, Cask Boilers, Platelayers, Stillions, Racking Shed and more, in this fiefdom that had discovered democracy. A new way of management was taking shape in the Brewery. The men who had struggled to be heard were now, through their union, meeting their bosses as equals. It was a revolution in how the Brewery worked and major challenges lay ahead.

Jack Carruthers emerged as one of the shop-floor champions. He was, by the time of this great change, Chief Shop Steward in the Cooperage Department. For Carruthers, originally sceptical about the WUI, his rank in the union came about through his criticism of it. While Larkin and Ferguson were trying to bring changes at the union/management level, Carruthers had been working to make changes within the union structure of the Brewery.

Jack wrote in his memoir:

> I became the Chief Steward of the Cooperage Department and this came about because of my strong criticism to the Branch Committee of the complete lack of organisation or control by the Union. I pointed out that in my department there were twelve shop stewards for 200 out of 500 men and that individually they were going to see the Manager who, because of lack of co-ordination and common policy among the shop stewards, played Ducks and Drakes with them and was able to use the famous British ploy of 'Divida et Impera' (divide and conquer).
>
> I convinced the Committee that one man, subject to them only, should control the shop stewards and be the only one to deal with the Manager in each department.
>
> If each department had a Chief Steward, all of whom sat on the Branch Committee, then a common policy and approach would be

assured, and if the Union showed the men that it was capable of succeeding in their efforts to rectify matters then more men would take courage and join the Union.

Needless to say, the WUI approached management at the end of the year in pursuit of something that had yet to be achieved: agreement to a union-led pay rise for the men.

On 16 January 1952 Harvey, Morrissey and the ubiquitous foreman Farnan (still maintaining the foremen's profile in these changing times) met Ferguson and employee Mick McGregor of Number Two Brewery section who was the elected Secretary of the WUI Brewery Branch. Ferguson presented the case that the cost of living had risen and that there was a round of pay increases happening around the city. He said the union was seeking an 11% pay rise. Harvey did not agree with the figures presented and offered – with no option of further negotiation – a rise of five shillings. The only compromise was that Harvey said rates could be considered again after six months. The game that Ferguson had explained was not played: there was no 'horse trading' and no opportunity for counter-proposals and counter-offers. The WUI held a general meeting of its Guinness members at which it was decided to accept the offer. It was a damp squib for such a key event: a non-trade man sitting opposite Sir Charles Harvey, a concession from management to a WUI bid for a pay increase. But these were crucial precedents in the changing dynamic between management and worker in the Brewery.

The next line of attack by the Union was a revision of what was seen as levels of skill in various non-trade jobs. What had been the faceless mass of non-skilled workers known only to their foremen by their staff number and not really known to management at all started to define themselves: their jobs, the risks taken in their working lives and the reality of their working conditions. Guinness Chief Engineer W. D. Robertson became the middle man between union and management in this revision of how the men would be perceived and paid. Men working in the 'scaffolding and slingers group', men in the Machinery Department, men in Cooperage, men in the Dried Grains Department, Drivers,

Barge and Crane Men. Jobs were being defined and upgraded. The negotiations were as much about conditions as about pay. The core theme was something that had been missing for too long: dignity.

Jack Harte also noticed another change: foremen started coming to him, as shop steward, to let him know when some work practice change or other issue was coming down the line so that the men would have advance warning and any possible problems could be discussed. Instead of the old way of the foremen keeping the concerns of the workers under wraps and passing only positive reports up the management line, they were now keen to prevent any confrontation with the workers as the union could now go to management.

Yet even as all this progress was being made, the union in the Brewery was having internal problems of two kinds: men were falling into arrears but – more seriously – a few shop stewards who were collecting the union dues were not passing the money on to the union. One such collector ran up a whopping £195 debt with the union (not far off an entire month's income for the union in the Brewery or a year's pay for a man at the bottom of the scale). The situation only came to light when Ferguson wrote to members warning them that they were in arrears and they wrote back saying they had been paying their dues regularly to this particular shop steward. Carruthers had to go to the man and confront him with the situation. He learned that the man had a gambling problem. An agreement was made whereby this man would pay back his debt at the rate of one pound ten shillings a week, but in fact he never honoured the debt and the union had to swallow the loss. Another shop steward, very popular with the men and very effective, was confronted by Jack Harte because he had not passed the union dues he had collected on to the union. This man, using his gift for negotiating, calmly responded to Harte: 'All right, how much of the money owed will you settle for?' Other shop stewards were removed from their union position and legal actions were threatened: one of them had turned the union payments he was collecting to entrepreneurial use as cashflow for buying and selling second-hand cars!

Jack Carruthers, meanwhile, was active in organising the union and motivating the men. He also wrote an open letter to his men reminding them of the value of their trade union and urging them to pay their dues:

> Your weekly contribution of one shilling entitles you to full and adequate protection if you are being unjustly treated, and to other important benefits, but it cannot make you a good Trade Unionist unless you fully understand the reason why your fellow workers cease to be 'mates' and become 'brothers' – members of one large family, ready to rally round you in times of need. Unity is strength and where there is strength your natural right to decent treatment compatible with your status as human beings and respect for the dignity of labour is assured.

In another of his many such motivational appeals he wrote: 'Let us all, Brothers, live up to the motto of the Workers' Union of Ireland, 'Each for all: all for each.' Not "every man for himself!"'

On the pay front, the WUI's pursuit of a broad sweep of pay rises for all in the Brewery was set aside as a matter for the national work of the trade unions while specifics that could only be known by the men doing the jobs were brought to the Board's attention. Late in 1952 the WUI presented a claim for a whopping 20 percent all-round pay rise for its members in the Brewery – a claim it agreed to delay while the tradesmen, who had not received a pay rise in over a year, finished their negotiations. In any event, an eight-shilling pay rise was offered by the Brewery to its non-trade workers and was accepted 'under protest'. The pay rise sought was a reflection of rising inflation in Ireland as it faced probably its most difficult decade in economic terms with growing unemployment and emigration.

In the Cooperage Department at the Guinness brewery, however, the men felt they had reason to celebrate. At a Christmas Eve event they gave their Chief Shop Steward Jack Carruthers 'a very suitable presentation'. They thanked him for 'the feeling of confidence in the future which his uncompromising adherence to Trade Union principles gave them and assured him of continued support in the New

Year'. There was plainly a strong bond between Jack and the men he represented and he was always highly regarded and very popular. It would have been a tough personal time for Jack – his mother died at the end of November and the Guinness Branch Committee recorded a Vote of Condolence for him in his bereavement, 'all members standing as a mark of respect'.

Bonding was going on at another level. Larkin received a letter from Harvey at the end of the year stating: 'The first of our two new Cross-Channel motor vessels "The Lady Grania" is due at Dublin on 1 January, 1953, after having completed her trials. We think you might be interested to come and look over her, and we are therefore arranging to receive guests aboard between 11AM and 1 PM on Monday, 5 January'.

At the start of 1953 there was a new but retrograde step taken when the Brewery management were informed: 'After some lengthy negotiations between themselves, senior Foremen amongst the Tradesmen and non-Tradesmen combined to form an Association which is to be called St James's Gate Brewery Senior Foremen's Association. Membership will be confined to the No. 1 and No. 2 Grade Foremen and the No. 1A and No. 1 Grade non-Tradesmen.' Mr M. Farnan, perhaps influenced by attending management meetings with representatives of the WUI, was Chairman of this Association. This was the same man who had been part of the original delegation to management back in 1946 complaining about the dangers of allowing the setting up of the Association of Brewery Employees. He had obviously seen the light. It was nevertheless an attempt at maintaining elitism, one of its goals being: 'to foster the interests of the Brewery and bring closer and more friendly co-operation between its members and the Board of Directors'. One of their first proposals was to remove the title of 'foreman' from any man below Grade 2. The Association also stated its wish to negotiate pay and conditions for its members: this trade union idea was catching on!

Mick McGregor had been one of the earliest supporters of the WUI in the Brewery and the first secretary of the Guinness Branch. Harte recalled how

The man who started it all: Arthur Guinness. Image courtesy of the Guinness Archive.

Labourers pose in groups in the Cooperage yard on lower level of St James`s Gate Brewery, c.1906. Image courtesy of the Guinness Archive.

The Guinness board-room. Sir Charles Harvey on left of frame. Finbarr Flood, who would become managing director, recalled once having the job of turning the pages of a large manual for Sir Charles. Image courtesy of the Guinness Archive.

Hard labour in the kieves, where Jack Harte worked. Image courtesy of the Guinness Archive.

W O R K E R S   U N I O N   O F   I R E L A N D

BREWERY (GUINNESS'S) SECTION.

5a College Street,
DUBLIN
4th July, 1949.

THINK   OVER   THIS !

(1) Before the War Brewery employees on the whole had better rates and conditions than those obtaining in outside employment.

(2) By utilising the machinery of Trade Union organisation the workers outside narrowed that gap, closed it and in some cases passed the Brewery level.

(3) Meanwhile the A. B. E. the only negotiating body then available to Brewery employees was finding it increasingly difficult to get any concessions whatever from the Board.

(4) The Board published a circular letter intimating it had no objection to their employees joining a Trade Union.

(5) The A. B. E. took the employees grievances to the Labour Court, where it was intimated the Board would prefer to deal with a recognised Trade Union, rather than negotiate with the internal staff organisation.

(6) The A. B. E. later found it impossible to make any headway with the Management, the latter making it clear they were only interested in problems of greater efficiency.

(7) The E. C. of the A. B. E. and the five departmental committees decide unanimously to summon a special meeting of members of the Association, to recommend its dissolution in view of the proven ineffectiveness of an internal organisation or "House Union" and to recommend the members should establish a branch of the Workers Union of Ireland.   By an overwhelming majority the members adopted the recommendation.

(8) A plebiscite is taken of the employees as to whether they desire to join "an outside" Trade Union.   The papers are distributed by Foremen and the official machinery of the Brewery is used to conduct the ballot thus conveying the impression the Board is responsible (subsequently the Board in reply to a letter from Deputy Larkin, General Secretary, disclaimed responsibility and reiterated employees were perfectly free to do as they wished).

(9) Despite the suggestion the Board was officially concerned with the plebiscite, of 2,500 or so employees competent to vote, only just over 1,000 did actually do so, that is two out of every five, and of these 800 or so voted against joining a legitimate Trade Union, or one in every three. Despite this it is alleged a majority voted for another internal Association.

(10) It is now suggested the Board is now prepared to negotiate on wages or conditions with the Works Committee. WHY? What factor has intervened causing such a change in policy? THE WORKERS UNION OF IRELAND ! ! !

A Workers' Union of Ireland publication aimed at stirring up the Guinness non-tradesmen. Image courtesy of the Guinness Archive.

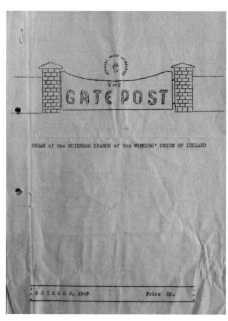

Home-made agitation. The cover of the 'Gatepost'. Image courtesy of the Guinness Archive.

James Larkin Jr. Image courtesy of the SIPTU Archive.

Denis Larkin.
Image courtesy of
the SIPTU Archive.

The fiery and dynamic
Christy Ferguson.
Image courtesy of the
SIPTU Archive.

The Guinness Dublin Board of Directors, 1959. Seated in front from left: Lord Moyne, the Earl of Iveagh and C. K. Mill. Standing at the back from left: Sir Charles Harvey, Sir Richard Levinge, Sir Alexander Ingleby-MacKenzie and Viscount Elveden. Image courtesy of the Guinness Archive.

Rolling out the barrels. Image courtesy of the Guinness Archive.

Jack Carruthers, Branch Secretary (1953-1969), WUI No.9 Branch, Guinness Brewery. Image courtesy of the Carruthers Family Collection.

The vast cooperage section, where Jack Carruthers worked. Image courtesy of the Guinness Archive.

A union meeting for the Traffic Department. From left of frame: Jack Carruthers, Jack Harte, Paddy Hoey (Chief Shop Steward), Tommy Carroll (Note-taker). Image courtesy of the Carruthers Family Collection.

WUI Union Parliament meeting in Dublin, 1954. Ferguson, the Larkin brothers and Carruthers are in the photo. Image courtesy of the SIPTU Archive.

The view out from St James's Gate to 98 James's Street, where Harvey and his family lived. Image courtesy of the Guinness Archive.

Major-General Sir Charles Offley Harvey. Image courtesy of the Guinness Archive.

Lt-General Sir Geoffrey Stuart Thompson, who succeeded Sir Charles. Image courtesy of the Guinness Archive.

Jack Harte presents Jack Carruthers with a gift on the event of Carruthers' resignation as Branch Secretary of the Workers' Union of Ireland No. 9 Branch. Left to right in frame is: C .H. E. Chamney, Manager, Planning and Development. Denis Larkin, General Secretary, WUI. Jack Carruthers. John Foster, General President, WUI. Jack Harte. Derek Carruthers. Paddy Cardiff, General Officer, WUI. Reg Hannon, Personnel Officer. J.N. Cairns, Brewery Manager. Image courtesy of the Carruthers Family Collection.

From left: Jack Carruthers, Vincent O'Hara and Mick Kiersey at a union congress in Tralee, 1954. Image courtesy of the Carruthers Family Collection.

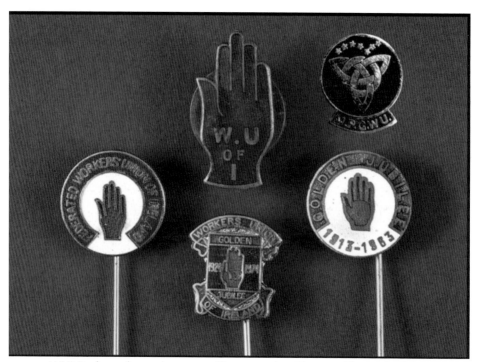

WUI Badges down the years. Photographer Tommy Clancy, badges property of Francis Devine.

The timber mount and latterhead design with Red Hand, WUI, and the Larkinite slogans. Image courtesy of the Irish Labour History Society.

WUI banner. Image courtesy of the Irish Labour History Society.

By 1946 when Harte, Carruthers and Harvey came to Guinness the brewery was producing 90 million pints a year. Image courtesy of the Guinness Archive.

The view from Sir Charles Harvey's home to the Brewery gates. Image courtesy of the Guinness Archive.

A presentation by Viscount Elveden to Jack Harte 'as a token of appreciation of his courage in rescuing a boy from the Liffey', published in the *Harp* Magazine Summer 1962 edition. Image courtesy of the Guinness Archive.

Jack Carruthers in later life. Image courtesy of the Carruthers
Family Collection.

Guinness being loaded in foreground, Liberty Hall in the background. Image courtesy of the Guinness Archive.

McGregor, devoted to the union cause, was always standing at the Brewery gate outside of working hours to hand out union literature and encourage the men to join the WUI 'hail, rain or snow'. But for all the progress McGregor would have seen, he plainly did not feel confident that Ireland would offer the best future for his family. After a bout of illness leading to surgery, he decided to quit the Brewery and his union work and emigrate to start a new life in Australia – though he returned to Ireland a few years later and (all due credit to the Guinness company for their liberal nature) was given back his job in the Brewery. He did not, however, get involved in trade union work again. McGregor's departure, late in 1953, created an opening for Branch Secretary and Larkin invited Jack Carruthers to meet him at his office at Thomas Ashe Hall. A few months earlier Jack, after attending a union conference, had written a piece for Larkin's trade union journal *Report*, with the title 'Blame the fellow who went to the Meeting!' in which he attacked apathy among trade union members who left the responsibility to others:

> We are never tired of repeating that we, the members, are the Union, but it does not look like it when one sees only a union official and a few loyal members at a meeting, because the majority are too apathetic to attend. We are all anxious to maintain our present standard of living and improve it if possible, but the majority of us stay away from the union meeting and leave it to the other fellow to decide how this is to be done. Of course, if something goes wrong we blame the other fellow, the fellow who attended the meeting, or better still, we blame the Union official.
>
> This is not good enough. If we want to be as good men as our fathers were, then we have got to take a real and proper interest in our Unions which they fought to establish, build up and strengthen so that they could hand them over to us for our protection and advancement. We say that we are the Union, well, if we are we had better get along to our Union meetings because if we don't attend there may be no meeting, aye, and some day we might wake up to find there was no Union, because the other fellow also forgot to attend or had something else to look after.

Larkin asked Jack to take on the job of Branch Secretary – the very job he outlined in his article as thankless or worse. But he took on this job as full-time

WUI trade union official for the Guinness brewery. Jack recalled: 'I said that I would as no one else would take the responsibility, even people outside the Brewery would not touch the job.'

One of the reasons that Larkin would have chosen Carruthers was that they were like-minded men. They were people who saw the bigger picture. Jack wrote of his new role: 'Being Secretary gave me the opportunity to influence the course I had mapped out in my mind for the kind of organisation it was necessary to create if the powerful Guinness management were to be brought into the 20th century.'

It was the start of the era of Jack Carruthers' influence on the Guinness brewery. One of the first focuses for this popular Chief Shop Steward turned Branch Secretary, though, was to turn his attention on his own union members: those who were not paying their subscriptions. Indeed, an ongoing theme in Jack's work would be putting pressure on those men who enjoyed the benefits of union membership without paying for their share in those benefits. He was concerned to see that the membership of the WUI in the Brewery was not growing but was stuck, he estimated, at about 1,190 – the inference being that there were men who had joined the union but did not pay their union dues.

Most of Carruthers' and Ferguson's correspondence with Guinness in these months concerned either individual cases or general concerns about working conditions. Pay increases were not on the agenda. This new combination of men – Carruthers now working with Ferguson and Larkin – was the start of a shift in relations between management and trade union. The main concern was about a better quality of life for the men in terms of promotions, working environment and recompense for shift work. In most cases, Harvey agreed to make the changes proposed by the union.

For its part, the WUI tried another approach to the matter of winning a pay rise for its men: proposing the notion of profit participation for all Guinness employees. An elaborate case was prepared, demonstrating that the Brewery was hugely profitable and the workers' pay should be gauged on that, rather than how their rates compared to those of other – less profitable – employers. Ferguson wrote to Harvey saying the pay claim would be based on 'the remarkably high profits of the Brewery'. Harvey replied that he would consider any proposal from the union, but that he saw 'no prospect of any rise in remuneration or any promise of any bonus'.

Ferguson's reply to this in September 1953, on behalf of the Branch Committee now headed by Carruthers, had the first tones of union sabre-rattling in a long time:

> (It is) quite clear to us that Management's conception of co-operation means in effect that the worker should give, where the Management requires effort of any kind, but that the Management on its part is not prepared to sympathetically co-operate with the workers.
>
> I am now to inform you that the Branch Committee will not co-operate with the Management in any of its projected schemes of re-organisation, introduction of new techniques or any other process leading to improved production or/and productivity.

Storm clouds were rumbling. Harvey considered his situation – knowing that the Brewery was in serious need of new technology and of new work practices to match it. In November, Harvey led a 'conference' of heads of departments in which he discussed plans for training for management. He wanted to set up a system of monthly meetings between department heads and staff, and between staff and foremen. Instructional films and lectures would also be used as a training tool, with the Brewery making its own films of the men at work. Harvey wanted to increase awareness among staff and foremen and was promoting such further measures as having brewery tours and inter-works visits where staff could visit other companies of similar scale. Probably his most novel idea was: 'it was felt that much benefit would be derived from new entrants in departments employing labour being made to carry out actual labouring jobs themselves on first joining their department'. It was all about improving relations between staff and worker as part of the new ethos triggered by the unionising of the Brewery.

Harvey became much more proactive in terms of industrial relations in the Brewery. Guinness had always encouraged learning for its workers and Harvey was now applying that philosophy to industrial relations within the Brewery. He had embraced the concept of open communication between management and the workers.

The relationship between Ferguson and Harvey was able to make the difference in terms of the union/management conflict that had developed. In November, Harvey wrote a letter to Ferguson saying: 'Thank you for the copy of the 'Christian Science Monitor' which I return herewith. I wish the relations between management and the Trade Unions were as mature in this country as they appear to be in New England. How easy your job and mine would be!'

The disagreement culminated in a 'conference' meeting of the main union figures with Harvey and a management line-up. Ferguson wrote to Jack Carruthers and Branch Chairman Mick Kiersey informing them of this conference set for 3 PM on 14 December and requesting them to meet him at 2.30 PM at the bus stop beside the Brewery.

Ferguson, Carruthers and Kiersey met Harvey, Morrissey and Chamney. There were three items on the agenda: a general pay rise, a review of the negotiation machinery between union and brewery and a raise in pay for very early morning work.

Harvey expressed the wish that the Branch Committee would withdraw its threat of not co-operating with improved technology and work practices and Ferguson replied that the union members were extremely angry and had wanted him to send management 'a strongly-worded letter, which somewhat to their annoyance he had softened down'. However, because the Brewery had issued profit-related end-of-year bonuses of four and a half weeks' wages to the men, Ferguson withdrew the pay claim, telling management that 'Guinness members of his Union were immature in Union ways'.

It was an extraordinary turn-around: over the years the workers had gone from struggling to have a say in pay and conditions to being reined in by the union that had fought for the right to represent them. It was a sign of the unexpected bond evolving between management and trade union. Things had come a long way since the days of mutual suspicion between all-powerful employers and 'Larkin's rabble'.

That was not the only surprise at this groundbreaking meeting: the walls between worker and management that had been such absolute barriers started to crumble. Ferguson wanted more direct access to heads of departments, even meeting them on a regular basis to routinely discuss brewery matters. Harvey agreed. Ferguson proposed streamlining communication between Senior Shop Stewards, the Branch Secretary and Heads of Departments – a move that gave Jack Carruthers much more direct authority on behalf of the union in the Brewery. Harvey agreed. Within days Sir Charles would issue a directive to the Heads of Departments setting all this in motion – and Carruthers stepped in immediately to shake up working conditions by pushing for changes in shift work arrangements and payments. It was the start of his very direct presence dealing with worker/management problems in the Brewery.

Bringing the meeting to a close Ferguson said he did not wish, at that time, to discuss the matter of rates of pay for early morning work. Harvey, however, offered an early morning allowance of time-and-a-half for work started before 6 AM, plus a shift allowance of one shilling and nine pence. This proposal would later be accepted by the workers.

Carruthers and Kiersey would have walked Ferguson back to his bus stop after the meeting. They might well have taken a diversion – Jack Carruthers once joked that he only started taking the occasional drink when he realised he usually bought Ferguson, on behalf of the men, a glass of whiskey after meetings. Maybe the three sat together reflecting on how readily Sir Charles was accepting the changes the WUI had brought to the Brewery.

As the year drew to a close, Ferguson wrote to Harvey to thank him on behalf of the workers for the bonus. He withdrew the threat of non-co-operation with work study, though added the caveat that: 'This is of course not to suggest, or to be understood in any manner whatever, as meaning or indicating that we must not have a discussion on the compensation to be paid to our members in the event of any increased production or productivity in consequence of any new machinery or productive organisation that may be devised. Despite the foregoing, however, my members really appreciate the help given them by the Board's decision.'

Harvey was happy to pass this letter on to Beaver, saying: 'There is no doubt that they all want to play with us, and the bonus gave them a very good face saver for withdrawing the silly letter they wrote last September.' Union/management relations were exceptionally good. The time had come for the next big change at Guinness: how the brewery itself functioned.

Six

Changes Brewing

On 7 October 1954 Sir Charles Harvey gave a talk to the Works Committee: the theme was Work Study. It was the start of the quietest revolution Harvey introduced to the firm. He started out by explaining that Sir Hugh Beaver had warned, five years earlier, that rising costs meant the company would be at risk if the market fell to pre-war levels. Beaver had issued a Board Order on Financial Control. Harvey explained there were two sides to this: budgetary control and cost control. The former was a matter of abiding by sound accountancy, the latter opened up a new world: Work Study. As he stated: 'cost control applies the technique of management to each and every cog of the machine, and by comparison of standards and actuals can check the use of materials and the utilisation of labour, plant and services, and can advise management regarding alternative processes or courses of action.'

This was the other side of the coin of change in the Brewery.

Harvey outlined how Work Study – which had evolved in the USA over the previous decades – functioned. It broke down into the components 'method study' and 'work measurement'. He described the former so:

> The record of what is being done or is proposed is generally made on a Process Chart and then each item on the chart is challenged with the questions WHY? WHO? WHEN? WHERE? HOW? etc. with a view to eliminating all that is unnecessary and then regrouping the essentials into the best possible sequence. The

Process Charts may record manual or material movements. It should be noted that Method Study is the prerogative and duty of management.

Extra pints of Guinness being doled out by the foremen to the workers for getting a job done more quickly would no longer be a measure or incentive for productivity. This new dissecting of tasks and processes, with its jargon of Work Units ('A Work Unit represents the amount of work which an average trained worker, on time work, is expected to perform in one minute; it contains a fraction of a minute of work, plus a fraction of a minute of rest.') and Time Study would be launched by Harvey in the following years. It was the start of the shift away from what was seen as an outdated, inefficient brewery structure towards modernisation at every level. Harvey noted that the aim was not to make people work harder, but to help them work more efficiently. He also noted that once the Work Units had been established it would be time to consult the trade unions: 'But that is a long way off, and until we have made a thorough survey of all the work in the Brewery and made up our minds where work measurement could be applied and have obtained the consent of the men to apply it, it would obviously be madness to lay down what form the incentive bonus is to take. All we can promise at this stage is that it is the intention of the Board that everybody connected with the firm, shareholders, employees and customers shall benefit both financially and otherwise from the great efficiency which we hope to achieve as a result of Work Study and Cost Control'.

Jack Carruthers was also a man who sought to introduce structure. In his early days with the WUI he had written to Larkin asking him to be specific about the role of a shop steward. He later created the role of Chief Shop Steward to smooth communication with management. He also, from the earliest days of his involvement in organising the union in the Brewery, developed an eighteen-point 'Guide for Shop Stewards' that showed the high standards he expected in the trade union movement:

1) Always be in possession of a Union Rule Book.
2) Read it frequently and familiarise yourself with its contents.

3) Have a working knowledge of the history of the Trades' Union Movement in general and the Workers' Union of Ireland particularly.

4) Become acquainted and understand the principles of Trade Unionism, and be always prepared to explain and defend them.

5) Where a principle is at stake, consult your Branch Committee or Chief Steward.

6) Be cordial and sympathetic to members seeking advice.

7) By example inspire the confidence in you that is so essential for the discharge of your duties.

8) In discussions with Foremen and others, if you are right and have the facts to prove it, then hold fast. If unsure give the other fellow the benefit of the doubt. Catch up on your knowledge later on.

9) Remember that to be aloof in the wrong way is fatal to true leadership, and will undermine effective team work.

10) Yours is an important position and a vital link in our organisation. Be proud of it and do not dishonour it.

11) Your Chief Steward has heavy responsibilities, help to ease them by your co-operation with him.

12) Be his extra eyes and ears. Keep him informed of matters connected with your section, and of actions requiring disciplinary measures. Always seek his advice before acting.

13) Negotiate to foreman level only, and be courteous and respectful. Do not remonstrate with him, but be firm and do not permit him to belittle your position.

14) If a complaint is not settled at Foreman level, report immediately to your Chief Stewards.

15) Submerge personal feelings towards those with whom you have to deal. Be impersonal and friendly with all.

16) Remember the qualities of leadership; Determination, Self-confidence, Courage, Integrity, Responsibility, Energy, Ability, Understanding.

17) Attend all Branch meetings when requested to do so.

18) In the eyes of Management your Chief Steward represents organised Labour in the Department. Respect his position and help strengthen his hand by observing his instructions, and by strict adherence to Trade Union principles. Reflect his strength and confidence in the future of the Workers' Union of Ireland.

But an early challenge for Jack Carruthers as Branch Secretary – and an unexpected blip just as it seemed industrial relations in the Brewery were exceptionally good – came from the very Guinness section he had worked in and had represented as Chief Shop Steward for years: the Cooperage Department. On 19 April 1955 some of the same men who had, a few years earlier, given him a Christmas gift in thanks for his representation of them went on unofficial strike.

It must have created divided loyalties for Jack – it certainly flared tempers within the union membership and gave ammunition to trade union cynics in management. There was also a clash between Carruthers and Ferguson. Jack wrote to Larkin on 22 April stating:

> I wish to protest in the strongest possible manner against the disgraceful attitude adopted by the National Organiser, Mr C. N. Ferguson, in attacking me in the presence of over 40 members of my Branch who were forced to witness an unjust chastisement (on Wednesday 20th April).
>
> His attack on me was based on the assumption that I was responsible for an article which appeared in the Press in regard to an unofficial stoppage in Guinness's when in fact I had nothing whatsoever to do with the report.

An article in the WUI *Report* magazine about Ferguson said: 'People fall out with Chris Ferguson and he is not always the last to pick a quarrel, but it soon passes over, because so many people have an affection for him.' This was certainly proven a week later when Carruthers wrote to Larkin:

> I now wish to withdraw the complaint … I have since discussed the matter with Mr Ferguson and now realise that his attitude towards me was as a result of a misunderstanding. As I have always enjoyed a friendly relationship with Mr Ferguson in the course of my Union work in the past I do not wish that relationship be hindered in any way.

The issue triggering the dispute reached a union/management meeting on 17 May, with Ferguson and Carruthers, along with shop stewards Savino, Byrne and Snedker facing a management line-up. The men's grievance was the lack of any promotion possibilities in their section. The head of the Cooperage Department was annoyed that despite the shop stewards' leading this unofficial strike, they were not reprimanded by their union. The matter was resolved in a compromise that the workers were not happy about – warning at the meeting that it could lead to further problems in the future. In a later exchange of letters, Ferguson assured Sir Charles Harvey that disciplinary measures would be taken against the shop stewards who had led, and taken part in, the unofficial action: though he would not reveal the action taken. Union/management life had become complicated.

Carruthers and the Guinness Branch Committee unanimously passed a resolution in May that Ferguson request a further pay rise from Guinness 'based on the difference in purchasing power with pre-war wages and in view of the very large profits of the company'. The General Executive Committee of the WUI considered this resolution and Larkin wrote to Carruthers in June with the GEC's view: the strategy was to pursue agreement from the Brewery that the bonus would be a regular annual event and that once the bonus had become established practice the WUI could seek a pay increase in conjunction with other unions in a nationally agreed structure. Ferguson had already told Harvey that the bonus was a far greater help to the families of the workers than a pay increase which tended to get absorbed into weekly life. The company, as part of the Federated Union of Employers, had also become more accustomed to dealing with the WUI in terms of the broader context of pay scales in Ireland and not just the Brewery. That in itself was another interesting change, considering that one of management's initial reasons for not wanting to see their men join a trade union was that they would be drawn into national union issues that would have nothing to do with the Brewery.

In July, however, the tables were turned when Guinness contacted the WUI saying they wanted a meeting to discuss a pay increase for its non-tradesmen. The building workers of Ireland had negotiated an increase and Guinness, through its membership of the FUE, had been informed of this. They wanted to keep their non-trade workers rate of pay in line with this increase.

Larkin, Ferguson, Carruthers and Kiersey met Harvey, Morrissey and Chamney in the Chairman's Room in the Brewery. Larkin set out a point he had been making for almost a decade: that the workers' wages had fallen behind the pre-war rates and an increase of 135 percent was needed to restore that value. It's hardly surprising that Harvey rejected that figure. He also did not want to enter into a process of trying to restore pay differentials between grades that had been eroded over the years of giving the same increase to all non-tradesmen. He offered an increase of eleven shillings per week for the lower grades and of 7.75 percent for higher grades.

Within days, the WUI called a meeting of its members at which this offer was discussed. While the offer was accepted, there was some outbreak of hostility when one union member (later accused of being a lapsed member) attacked Ferguson for his lack of negotiation skills. The scene must have been quite ugly as Ferguson later received letters of sympathy from other Guinness WUI men at the meeting and an official apology from Carruthers on behalf of the Guinness Branch Committee stating: 'We regret very much the discourteous manner adopted towards you by one of our members and we wish to disassociate ourselves completely from the comments made.'

Giving his annual report on 1955 at the Annual General Meeting of the Guinness Branch in February 1956, Jack Carruthers said he was: 'pleased to tell you that the past year has been a very successful one from many points of view, not only has membership been greatly increased but due to the tremendous efforts of your Committee, Chief Stewards and Shop Stewards the position of our Union in the Brewery has been greatly strengthened and consolidated.'

Membership stood at 1,900 – though again Carruthers lamented that there were still too many in arrears with their union dues and too few attending branch meetings.

Early in 1956, the forty-five WUI shop stewards in the Brewery joined to form their own Shop Stewards' Association. The Association had monthly meetings to improve communication within their ranks and to bring in guest speakers: in February Donal Nevin, research officer of the ITUC, gave a talk about 'Work Study and the attitude of trade unions to increasing productivity'. He could clearly see what was happening:

> For a long time workers have been subjected to a barrage of exhortations from all quarters about the necessity for raising productivity. Workers have not been slow to note the blatant contradiction between these exhortations and the continued failure of our economy to provide full employment for our population notwithstanding the loss of nearly three quarters of a million people through emigration since the State was set up.
>
> The fundamental attitude of workers to measures aimed at raising industrial productivity through work study has been determined by their bitter experience of unemployment and the emigrant ship. For apart from the fear of redundancy for themselves, workers must have regard also to the overall employment position in the country and the prospects of their sons and daughters being able to get work in their own country.

Nevin pointed out the balance between increased productivity leading to both higher wages and reduced employment. He warned that work study should be observed with caution by the unions, even though the trade union movement was not against the work study process. He also pointed out that, according to official statistics from the Central Statistics Office, output per wage earner had risen by 30 percent since before the war.

Jack Carruthers' rise to Branch Secretary coincided with changing times for the Guinness brewery. With its bicentenary approaching, the plant was being modernised. A bigger challenge was the marketplace: light beers were now out-selling dark beers such a Guinness. For the first time in its history the 'pint of plain' was falling out of favour with the working man on the international market and the popularity of ales and lagers was on the rise. Younger men preferred the simpler taste of lighter beers. Guinness was a one-product company and had to decide how it would respond. Not that the company was struggling to survive: net profits were running at over two million pounds a year.

Ireland, meanwhile, was going through a decade of relentless inflation and decline: the only areas of growth were emigration, unemployment and discontent. In May 1954 de Valera's Fianna Fáil minority government fell and was replaced by the 'second inter-party government' (Fine Gael, Labour and Clann na Talmhan). De Valera had maintained a vision of a rural and insular Ireland that was causing much of the decline and the new government showed no new thinking to reverse the downward trend, heading instead into an unpopularity that would see them fall before completing their full term. Guinness, despite the changing marketplace, still shone as one of the great Irish successes in an otherwise bleak economy.

An unexpected diversification came out of a chat Beaver had with friends on a hunting party. Someone asked which game bird flew the fastest and no one could come up with the definitive answer. Beaver followed up on the idea of there being a book that would officially research and record such facts. He was recommended to hire the twin brother journalists Norris and Ross McWhirter, and so *The Guinness Book of Records* was born. It was originally planned as a corporate gift but when launched it made its own record, becoming the biggest-selling copyrighted book ever, out-sold only by such books as the Bible. Quite an unexpected bonus for a company whose beverage was losing some of its following and whose Dublin brewery was in need of a major overhaul.

The company policy regarding trade union membership in the Dublin brewery had always been clear: recognise a trade union if it represented a majority of the non-trade workers but abide by the rule that no worker should be pressured to join the trade union and any worker's grievance could be heard by management whether or not the approach was made through the trade union. Jack wanted more than that. He wanted the position that had already been stated by Sir Hugh Beaver in the Park Royal Guinness plant as far back as 1948: 'All the labour in the Brewery belongs to the Transport and General Workers' Union. In view of this fact it has, for some considerable time past, been the Company's policy only to take on in the Brewery, union labour or labour that is willing to join a union.'

In March 1956, as a further part of the bridge-building James Larkin sought, an agreement was reached between the ITGWU and the WUI that no member of one union could change to membership of the other union without notification of their original union. The unions agreed that they would not accept a new member who was in arrears with the other union or who was taking part in an unofficial strike. It solidified the membership of each union: a bit like the adage 'good fences make good neighbours'. A joint statement from the two unions said: 'It is felt that the agreement will contribute very significantly towards establishing better trade union organisation generally; will make for better relations between these two powerful organisations, and will help to further discourage unofficial strikes.'

In the same month, Ferguson requested a meeting with Guinness management to discuss a revision of the existing agreement: 'The Workers' Union of Ireland is now truly representative of all non-trades workers in the Brewery. Consequently the Union wishes that all new men employed by Guinness should be members of the Union with whom the Board negotiates on behalf of the majority of workers.'

Harvey did not set an immediate date for this meeting, instead turning to the London office for advice. One of the chiefs there, N. B. Smiley, wrote to him: 'It seems wrong that men should be forced to join the union if they do not wish to do so. Nevertheless, facing the facts as they are here, I feel that we are in a better position negotiating with a well-supported Union than we would be if we had to deal with hot-heads not subjected to Union influence.'

Relations between Guinness and the WUI had developed well over the years since the Union had first made its presence felt in the Brewery. Cecil Chamney, manager of the Administrative Department and a man who had often chaired union/management meetings, expressed the view: 'I think we tend to listen to Shop Stewards more readily than to foremen and ought to remedy this.' His opinion was, of course, true. The rise of a unified voice for the workers brought an equal and opposite fall of unquestioned authority for the foremen. Sir Charles Harvey had to weigh up both sides of the argument. It was not a matter of whether or not the WUI would be recognised – it was the fear of Guinness becoming a trade union 'closed shop'.

The policy document drawn up by the Guinness side in preparation for the meeting listed the limitations it required the WUI to accept: no one could be pressured to join a trade union and grievances could still be heard without union involvement. In Park Royal, all but one man had joined the trade union and his right to remain so was upheld by management. In the meantime, however, pressure was coming from the other side. A meeting was held in the Rathmines Town Hall at which managers and supervisors discussed the changing landscape. The management representative Dempsey 'accepted a criticism that foremen were rarely informed where they were going by management'.

The planned union/management meeting, held at 3 PM on 3 April, was headed by Ferguson and Carruthers on the WUI side and Harvey and Morrissey on the Guinness side. It was an unusual meeting in that aside from one issue – the matter raised by Jack Carruthers of regrading for the shivers in the Cooperage Department (which Harvey in his office memorandum described as a 'hardy annual') – the matters being dealt with focused on the nature of the relationship between the union and Guinness management.

The first topic for discussion was 'The New Agreement'. Ten years on from the start of the struggle for union recognition for non-trade workers in the Brewery, Ferguson began presenting the WUI side by saying that the union 'had difficulty in exercising discipline as their members had threatened or might threaten to leave WUI and join another union.' His position, as reported in the minutes of the meeting, was that sole recognition for the WUI would mean 'that management would not be disrupted by minorities breaking away and causing trouble. The men would still be free to join another union if they wished, but only in an orderly manner.'

Ferguson recognised the right of Guinness to select those they chose to employ, and he accepted that older men in the Brewery would not be obliged to join the union, but he sought that no new employee could start work until he had joined the WUI.

Harvey again expressed his disagreement – standing by the view that it was wrong to force a man to join a trade union. He thought it might even be unconstitutional. He then read out the company's proposed wording for the 'New Agreement' with the WUI: 'Selection of employees will remain solely at the discretion of Management and it will not be a condition of employment that men shall belong to a Union. On the other hand, every man joining for employment on the non-tradesmen's list will be advised to join a Union and will be told that the Union with which we negotiate is at present the Workers' Union of Ireland'.

Ferguson agreed to accept the compromise, subject to confirmation by the Brewery Branch Committee. It was, after all, a small verbal dance that gave both sides what they wanted while giving neither side the upper hand. It was a perfect example of how union and management had learned to understand each other: a mature give and take.

The next topic, presented by management, was effectively their mirror proposal. Harvey wanted to formalise the structure of communication between shop stewards and management as he said there had been a growing tendency to 'short-circuit the foremen': something that had long been a concern as the union had grown in strength. Harvey set out the levels of communication to be agreed:

(a) Shop Steward to Foreman.
(b) Chief Shop Steward to Departmental Manager.
(c) (i) Secretary, Brewery Branch to Manager,
Administrative Department (informal approach).
(ii) H.Q. Workers' Union of Ireland to the Board.

Ferguson and Carruthers agreed that this was the correct structure and Harvey said he would issue a memo to this effect to junior officials and management.

This meeting was a turning point. When Christy Ferguson wrote to Sir Charles Harvey a week later confirming that the Branch Committee accepted the proposed wording of 'The New Agreement' he added: 'I take this opportunity to thank you for the atmosphere of co-operation which made it possible for us to easily and expeditiously negotiate the modified agreement.' Jack Carruthers later wrote of the event: 'This final move consolidated our by now formidable strength and established us as "the most powerful and sophisticated Union Branch in the British Isles" (Quote Jim Larkin 1957)'. For his part, Harvey issued notices about the Brewery's recognition of the WUI and about the structure of communication between management and union. Both sides were growing and both sides were learning. The unlikely marriage had turned into a grand success.

Soon after this move Harvey wrote an internal memo saying he was 'not entirely satisfied that everybody who deals with labour fully understands all the rules regarding conditions of employment and overtime. I have therefore asked Mr Morrissey to give a talk in the first instance to those concerned on the upper level'.

The talk was given in the Green Room of the Rupert Guinness Hall. Morrissey outlined the amenities and rights of the employees and gave a history of labour relations in the Brewery. He was proud to state there had never been a strike in the Brewery and reminded his listeners of all the comforts – welfare, job security and so on – enjoyed by the workers. He gave a short history of the Labour movement in Ireland – skipping over any mention of the Lockout. He also repeated the old Guinness myth: 'The fact that our men did not organise into a union until so recently was due to the good relations and treatment which employees have always received from the company.'

The changes brought by the 'New Agreement' were not without their problems, however. In August, Harvey wrote to Larkin to complain about a matter that had been brought to his attention: four men in the Racking Section had refused to join the WUI and were being 'sent to Coventry' by the other men who would not speak with them. He reported that Carruthers had been approached about the issue by Morrissey and had said that he knew nothing officially about it but had heard unofficially. Jack Carruthers had said that: 'the men had a perfect right to refuse to speak to any other man if they so desired, and he was not prepared to interfere.' Harvey protested that the action of the union members was against the spirit of the union/management agreement.

The following month, at a union/management meeting, Ferguson brought up the issue of an incident when a manager had refused to meet Branch Secretary Jack Carruthers about something concerning him. Harvey and Carruthers clashed – Harvey saying that 'the subject the Branch Secretary wished to discuss was merely based on rumour and had nothing to do with him.' When Jack Carruthers insisted that the matter – promotions in the Cooperage Department – was indeed relevant to him, Harvey made the comment that perhaps the job of Branch Secretary was becoming full-time and Carruthers should work outside the Brewery. In fact, as the rate of change in the Brewery accelerated and with it the demands on the time of the Branch Secretary, Guinness provided an office space that he could work from on site to help expedite dealing with any labour problems that arose. The conflict between the two men passed.

Harvey continued his process of changing the culture of labour relations within the Brewery. One staff course on the subject gave an overview of the work conditions for Guinness employees and emphasised: 'The necessity of treating all men, irrespective of rank, as human persons entitled to full respect and consideration, until, by any act of theirs, they forfeit the right to such respect and consideration.'

A new area of tension – and a new need for the two sides to keep communicating – was the arrival on the brewery floor of work study. There was now a Work Study Department, headed by Brewer W. A. D. Windham assisted by Messers R. J. Law, E. A. Conway and S. G. Bennett who were Work Study Officers. This was an independent department reporting directly to Harvey. Its terms of reference, as described in an article written later by Law, were: 'to act in an advisory capacity to the Board and to Heads of Departments for the detailed investigations of matters relating to the more effective use of manpower, raw materials and capital equipment.' The services of the department were available on request only, and the results of any such study requested would be given to the head of department who had requested to see them. The department also gave regular two-week courses for management in which the principles of work study were taught – including the looming theme of Job Evaluation – and culminated in the Tour of the Brewery and, the Work Study Department not being above its own principles, a final discussion about the course and 'Criticisms of Course'.

The problem for the workers, and the WUI, was that management had started into this without first informing the union but when the union became aware of it and complained, Harvey immediately arranged for Branch Chairman Mick Kiersey to meet Brewer Windham. At that meeting Windham expressed his surprise at the complaint as he believed workers were always informed in advance of a work study session. A routine was agreed between both sides whereby lines of communication would be open from before the process to the analysis after the process. It was a very open and admirable approach to this interaction between management and worker and the union agreed with the importance of the process. Windham also agreed to arranging films about the work study process to be shown in the Rupert Guinness Hall as a way of helping the workers understand what was involved. As the notes on the meeting summed it up: 'It was pointed out that in order to meet the severe competition existing today, it was essential to make full use of up-to-date methods such as Work Study. By their use it was hoped not only to maintain our trade but to increase it, which was clearly in the interest of all employees.' These were still early days in what would become a major issue.

Jack Carruthers wrote to Sir Charles Harvey at the end of 1956 wishing him and the Board of Directors, 'on behalf of the Branch Committee and our members', an enjoyable Christmas and a prosperous New Year. No one could foretell the huge changes to come in the new year.

Christy Ferguson, the National Organiser who had been such a major driving force for the WUI, died on 4 February 1957 at the age of fifty-two. He was a widower and had been in very poor health, suffering from cardiac and bronchial problems for several years. His death was a huge loss to the union; not only had he been a key figure in the unionising of Guinness and the growth of the WUI, he had also been filling the gap at the top of the union caused by James Larkin's continuing work as a TD. The following month Jack Carruthers, giving his annual address as Branch Secretary, referred to Ferguson as 'our guide and counsellor when the awakened workers of our firm united to form the Guinness Branch of the Workers' Union of Ireland in 1949.'

Looking back on his own third full year as Branch Secretary, Jack again lamented the lack of attendance at union meetings (records show he was the only man on the twenty-six member Branch Committee to attend every one of their twenty-six meetings in the year) and urged the union members to pay their dues and respect their shop stewards. He could look back on a good year in which there had been no major disputes. But he also flagged the emerging challenges of Job Evaluation: 'As this subject is too involved, I do not propose to raise it here today except to assure all our members that we are not committed to anything nor will they be committed without having an opportunity of fully discussing its implications. You have no reason to distrust the leadership of this Union and you can rest assured that your interests will be closely guarded. I say this because I am aware of the false prophets spreading discontent among you. You should treat them with the contempt they deserve.'

The grade structure as it existed in the Brewery had been created by management with no consultation with the workers and, over the years of the evolving work of the WUI, it became impossible to find ways to upgrade workers in some areas and thereby improve their pay. Sir Charles Harvey had then proposed that a formal evaluation of every man's job should be carried out, as had been done in

Park Royal. After committee discussions, it had been decided to send Carruthers and Kiersey to Park Royal in early 1957 to meet fellow trade unionists there and to meet the men, a Mr Fontain and a Mr Black, who had carried out the job evaluation. Having had thorough discussions at Park Royal, where all expressed satisfaction with the changes made and the impartiality of the team, Carruthers and Kiersey then recommended to their Branch Committee that the job evaluation process be accepted. But with two provisos: the union reserved the right to challenge the final results of the team, and the union turned down the offer to have a representative on the team 'wishing to be completely free to criticise any or all of the final proposals'.

Two other important points were proposed by the WUI: that no employee's earnings would be reduced as a result of job evaluation and that no change arising from job evaluation would be put into operation prior to trade union agreement. Harvey accepted the latter point and did a diplomatic dodge on the former.

Fontain and Black had also attended a meeting of the Shop Stewards' Association at which they attempted to further clarify the neutrality of the Job Evaluation process. Fontain referred to the old method of seeking to have a job valued. This, he said, 'often led to long arguments before finally reaching agreement and equally often led to the more aggressive group or fellow getting the improvement at the expense of the more gentle element. . . . Continuing, Mr Fontain said that he must start at the bottom and work up, defining degrees of skill and responsibilities as he did so, and placing a higher monetary value on better quality work involving greater skill.'

The coalition government collapsed and the country went to the polls again – but this time Larkin stepped down as TD, realising he needed to devote all his energies to the WUI now that he no longer had Ferguson at his side. The results of the general election were that Fianna Fáil, still led by de Valera, came back into power with a clear majority. Seán Lemass was his second-in-command as Tánaiste.

Now firmly at the helm of his union, Larkin decided that he wanted to consolidate the WUI's position in the Guinness brewery. He sought to take the already-established recognition of the WUI as the official union representing non-trade workers one step further: to make paid-up membership of the union a condition of employment. This would have many consequences, not least giving the union the ultimate threat to a worker not paying his union dues that he could lose his job. Harvey was not against this move, but he sought detailed managerial and legal advice before he responded; there was always the danger that the last stand for Guinness as employers would be lost, namely that they had final say on who they decided to hire. It could also become a straitjacket preventing the hiring of seasonal workers and could create a conflict for such workers as the brewery police. Basically, though, it could also be an unfair imposition of union power.

The legal advice was that the company was entitled to make trade union membership a condition of employment for new employees but that those already in the company's employ could not be obliged to join.

Harvey requested, and the WUI presented, a list of the Union's members in the Brewery and Harvey initiated a mammoth process whereby every member would be interviewed to confirm that he was indeed in the Union and that he understood the implications of the proposed new arrangement. Harvey ruled out making trade union membership compulsory for employees in the Brewery, saying their work contract pre-dated any such agreement and had to be respected. The interview would serve the purpose of clarification. He wrote to Larkin:

> We cannot delegate any other body to alter the conditions of our employment on our behalf. We feel therefore that it is essential for us to interview each man who is on your list as a member of your Union and ask him to confirm that he is a member and understands the new arrangement.
>
> I feel sure that you yourself and Messrs Kiersey and Carruthers would take it for granted that our interview with each man was straightforward, but in order to remove any future possible suspicions that the interview was biased, we would be quite agreeable to allow a Shop Steward or anybody else appointed by the Branch Committee to be present as an observer when the men are being interviewed by their Departments.

This exchange led to a new official notice issued by Harvey in the Brewery under the title 'Conditions of Service of non-Tradesmen employed by Messrs Arthur Guinness Son and Co (Dublin) Ltd, at St James's Gate, Dublin, as affected by Trade Union Membership'. Larkin also issued an official notice from the WUI side making the same statement. With the agreed exceptions of seasonal workers, gate checkers, brewery police, technical assistants and those who reached Grade 1 as foremen, union membership became a condition of employment. As Larkin wrote in his notice:

> From September 'the Gate' becomes a union job and the members of the Workers' Union of Ireland will be asked to set the example in the new era they have brought about. In the meanwhile, and before 1 January, any members of the Workers' Union of Ireland who may be in arrears should make a special effort to get the arrears cleared so as to start with a clean sheet.

Larkin praised the achievement, calling it 'the culmination of eight years' work by the Union and its active members in the Brewery to firmly establish Trade Union organisation in St James's Gate Brewery. This great achievement is the result of the loyalty and adherence to Trade Union principles manifested by the 2,300 members of the Workers' Union of Ireland in the Brewery; and to the energetic and inspiring work of the Branch Officers, Branch Committee and Shop Stewards.

Larkin wrote to Harvey saying: 'we consider that the Board have approached and dealt with this whole matter in a very fair manner and that their attitude will be a major contributory factor to the continuance of good and harmonious relations in the Brewery.' Another development was a perfect symbol of this closer alliance between union and management. Larkin wrote to Harvey requesting that the union be allowed to set up its own noticeboards in the various sections of the Brewery for posting any union information. Harvey replied that he would prefer to redesign management noticeboards already in use so that one half would be for management notices and the other half for trade union notices: side by side. It was another remarkable change in union/management relations.

The ink was hardly dry on the union membership agreement when Larkin again raised problems caused by how men were promoted in the Brewery. Harvey arranged a 'conference', in which Larkin, along with Carruthers and Kiersey, could meet 'heads of large departments employing labour'. These heads explained the promotion process to Larkin: and it boiled down to the fact that no notification was given of upcoming vacancies, the promotions were made at the managers' discretion and seniority was not a deciding factor. While stressing that he did not consider promotions to be an area in which the Union could have a say, Larkin asked for some measures to be taken to make the process more transparent. Harvey stood by his opinion that the system was working. It would take a major showdown in the Brewery before that view changed.

As union/management communication became more regularised, the Registry Department that had existed, before all these changes, to record the numbers and the work records of nameless non-skilled workers transformed its philosophy and methods to match the changing times. In December 1957 the Guinness brewery's personnel chief, Cecil Chamney, issued a 'Guide to Labour Relations' to members of supervisory staff. It was so breezy and bright, glossing over certain union/management struggles, that it is worth quoting extensively and probably should be read to the accompaniment of the British *Movietone News* music of the era:

> There is traditionally an atmosphere of mutual trust and respect between the men employed in the Brewery and those who are in positions of authority over them. These notes are designed to assist you to preserve and strengthen these ties.
>
> Relationships between employer and employed in industry have changed greatly in the last ten years, but it is well to bear in mind that most amenities for employees, of which the modern firm boasts, have existed in the Brewery for fifty or more years. Our employee services have been a model to, and not imitation of, other firms.
>
> In 1948 the Board decided that they must keep abreast with the times, and that the old feudal system on which Guinness had flourished no longer appealed to modern young men. They decided, therefore, that it would be best to negotiate on controver-

sial matters with a recognised body, possessed of all the experience
and sense of responsibility expected from a modern trade union.

You should know all the men in your section. . . . You will learn
about the family worries of men; uncertainty about well-being of
children, financial worry etc is often the cause of a surly grunt at
6 am in the morning. . . . Never forget that each man is an
individual, and though employed by us is not owned by us. . . . The
exercise of authority in the Brewery has always been a gentle one. If
there is any doubt, the men always get the benefit of it. Even
in proved cases of breaches of regulations, judgement is always
influenced by consideration of circumstances.

It was an admirable philosophy from an evolving company that could still
consider itself the best employer in Dublin, if not in Ireland. One case handled
between the Company and the Union is a perfect example of its behaviour.
A labourer in the Brewhouse was caught pilfering (this almost always meaning
drinking the brew from a tap without permission) and was, in accordance with
company rules, fired on the spot. Larkin and Carruthers went to Harvey to
intercede for the man, who had a drink problem. Larkin made an appointment
for the man to be assessed by a psychiatrist who confirmed he was an alcoholic.
In light of this, Harvey agreed that the man be reinstated and put on sick pay
while receiving treatment in St Patrick's Hospital. When discharged from hospital
the man would be further assessed and if all seemed in order he could work in the
Brewery again – though not in the Brewhouse.

Windham was continuing his policy of openness and information regarding
Work Study in the Brewery and he wrote to Larkin inviting him: 'for lunch with
our Work Study Course for Staff on Monday 17 February. As before, it will start
with sherry at 1.10 pm.' It was a policy established by Harvey to ensure that this
process did not alarm the workers: there were regular 'appreciation courses' for
shop stewards, foremen, staff and workers. More departments were requesting the
services of Work Study, and R. J. Law, when writing about this, listed such areas
of study as: 'Maintenance of Cask Washing Machines; Transfer of Grist from
Robert Street to No. 2 Brewery; Collection and Sorting of Brewery Mail;

Cask Handling at Trade Department Stores'. The waves lapping on the beach had not yet been perceived by the Union as eroding the coast.

At the annual general meeting of the WUI Guinness members early in 1958, Carruthers celebrated the Union Shop Agreement that had come into effect: 'It can be our proud boast, that the impregnable fortress of St James's Gate has well and truly crumbled before the onslaught of organised labour, and it shall once again become an impregnable fortress, but this time to non-Union labour!' Carruthers also called for a silent prayer for Chris Ferguson 'whose leadership led us along the long and hard road to ultimate victory'.

Giving his annual report, Carruthers said WUI membership in the Brewery was 2,360 with only a small minority not in benefit. There were sixty shop stewards. Able to look back on a year of no major disputes and many successes, Carruthers thanked the many trade unionists who had worked with him, in particular two who were retiring: Jack Behan and Patrick Bruce. Ending the report he added: 'In conclusion I would like to propose a special vote of thanks to my better and more intelligent half, our esteemed Branch Chairman, Brother Michael Kiersey, whose courage helped to form the Union in the Brewery and whose devotion to duty has largely contributed to its present formidable position.' It was a well-deserved triumphant speech, so much having changed for the Brewery's general workers.

Larkin now turned his attention again to an old target: the annual bonus. He wrote to Harvey outlining his case for making it a guaranteed annual event instead of the uncertainty that had always surrounded it. The amount itself could go up and down depending on the Company's trading performance, but Larkin also pointed out the new working methods were creating bigger profits for the Brewery but were not being reflected in pay or bonus. Larkin claimed that if the annual bonus was formally established and a specific date of payment set, it would 'remove the present uncertainty which in itself is harmful to good industrial relations.'

Harvey and the Board, however, turned Larkin's suggestion down. Sir Charles replied to the letter stating that there were too many uncertainties – not least being that the St James's Gate brewery was only part of a number of subsidiary companies owned by the Parent Company and profits for it alone could not be treated separately. The bonus and, if it was awarded, the sum involved would continue to be uncertain. The only concession was that Harvey could see the possibility of bonuses being awarded as a result of higher productivity achieved through Work Study. It would take a while for the Union to realise just how passionate Harvey was about this new industrial concept.

For all the improvements in communication between management and the WUI, there was one issue on which negotiations failed and they had to resort to help from the Labour Court. The difference was over the method of promotion in the Brewery. The matter would drag on until almost the end of the year. But a far bigger issue was looming: as Guinness was using new work methods and machinery, it was starting to shed workers. It was also planning on closing down the Maltings unit at Cooke's Lane and integrating the workers from there into the main brewery site. Union and management agreed a formula for transferring men from one section to another, while keeping their grades, and for redundancy and early retirement. Slowly, for the union, the penny dropped: Work Study was the management side of the industrial relations revolution happening in the Brewery.

As worries mounted among the men Larkin suggested, and Harvey agreed, holding a 'conference' at which, again, senior management would meet senior trade union representatives to clarify the plans Guinness had for the Brewery. Larkin reported back that this was a healthy process and should be repeated regularly. Harvey decided, instead, to resuscitate the sidelined Works Committee as a way of passing information on production changes down the line from management to heads of department to the men on the floor who could decide if anything needed the involvement of the Union. He was determined to maintain some purpose for that structure.

The pint of Guinness had changed over the two centuries since its introduction to its appreciative drinkers. Arthur Guinness first produced a dark porter that evolved into Guinness Stout. Pulling a pint of draught Guinness was an art – and devoted drinkers would flock to particular pubs where the barman had mastered that art. It was a delicate process of filling the pint glass from two wooden casks: one above with the brew and one below with the carbonisation that gave the pint its creamy head. In 1956 company boss Sir Hugh Beaver commissioned the engineer Michael Ash to come up with a way of producing a consistently perfect pint. The task was named 'The Draught Project' but nicknamed in the Company 'The Daft Project' as it seemed completely impossible. Ash, however, came up with a solution in 1958 that would later be improved upon to ensure a perfect pint every time: a metal cask containing a section for the stout and a section for the mixture of carbon dioxide and nitrogen. It was called the 'Easy Serve'. This new process, of course, brought more change to the Brewery. Yet not all were convinced that the new system really was perfected and while some suggested that it be launched to tie in with the Guinness bicentenary in 1959, it was released only in England that year and not in Ireland.

After the loss of Ferguson, Larkin had more regular contact with his various Branch Secretaries. For Christmas 1958 Jack Carruthers sent him a gift of the *Guinness Book of Records*. In a letter of thanks Larkin wrote:

> May I say that our relationship during the period since Christy Ferguson's death has been both pleasant and fruitful. We both appear to have succeeded in establishing a friendly relationship, based on mutual confidence, and whatever little assistance I have been able to give to you has been more than equalled by the manner in which you have been able to advise me and keep me clear of difficulties and trouble.

Immediately after his father's death, Larkin had openly called for unity between the unions. Through discussions with John Conroy, head of the ITGWU, agreement was reached so that the two congresses that had been created through one of the many battles between O'Brien and 'Big Jim' could reunite into the Irish Congress of Trade Unions in 1959. The discussions culminated in a three-day conference held in Dublin at which Larkin had negotiations with representatives of the many unions that would be coming back together under one banner. Jack Harte, with colleagues William Gibson and Vincent O'Hara, were Guinness branch delegates to the conference. When full agreement was reached, Conroy became the first president of the new ICTU. It meant at last that the trade unions could speak with one voice when negotiating with government and employers. It was a perfect example of the difference between father and son: 'Young Jim' always put the issues ahead of personalities.

Unemployment and emigration remained a serious problem for Ireland as the Fifties came to an end. Seán Lemass, finally out from the shadow of de Valera, was Taoiseach of a country that had fallen economically behind the rest of Europe: British workers earned 40 percent more than Irish workers. Lemass invited the new ICTU into discussions on a new economic plan for Ireland based on a report by T. K. Whitaker in the Department of Finance. The country would cease to be built on the model of the farmer being the engine of the nation's economy and would look instead to industrial growth. It was the start of a process that would finally bring the country into the modern world de Valera had turned his back on.

In early 1959 Larkin submitted his – more or less annual – letter to Harvey seeking a pay increase. There had already been a national agreement for an increase of ten shillings per week but Larkin sought a further seventeen shillings (a sign of the times, he requested the rise 'for adult male employees, with proportionate increases for female and juvenile') to reflect the rise in the cost of living. As Larkin also commented, 'the Company can afford the increase claimed'. Indeed, the Company's annual profits had doubled to almost four million pounds in the years from 1953 to 1958.

Harvey responded after discussions with the Board. While not seeing a cost-of-living basis for an increase, the Board acknowledged: 'the promise they made when introducing Work Study: that it was their intention that shareholders, customers and employees should all benefit as a result of improved methods.' The decision was to offer a raise of ten shillings a week.

Larkin put this to a vote at a general meeting and it was rejected by the men. When he informed Harvey of this he arranged for a meeting but also presented a barrage of facts and figures to support his case. Harvey, prior to the meeting, fired back an even more impressive set of facts and figures and stated that the offer would not be increased. He had plainly never taken to the 'horse trading' concept Ferguson had tried to explain to him. In the event, the men agreed to accept the ten shilling raise.

At the 1959 general meeting of the WUI's Guinness Branch Jack Carruthers gave his annual report. He started his review of the year by reporting that membership was still rising, now having reached 2,508. He described the Branch as 'second to none in Ireland, North or South'. While it had been another relatively peaceful year of industrial relations in the Brewery, Carruthers noted that redundancy was becoming a significant issue and cause for concern as new machinery and work practices came along.

In this last year of the decade, a man who had been one of the leaders of the Labour movement in the Guinness brewery decided to step down. Mick Kiersey had been one of the founders of the Association of Brewery Employees and had, when the transition to the WUI happened, automatically become Chairman of the Guinness Branch. He had worked with McGregor and later with Carruthers, but after almost fifteen years devoted to establishing a voice in the Brewery for the workers he had become a foreman and there was a feeling his loyalties might be divided – even though he and Carruthers worked very well together. Another shop steward stepped forward to compete for the job of Chairman: Jack Harte. Although he and Carruthers knew each other through the Branch Committee, Carruthers didn't fully trust Harte and canvassed against him. Harte won the election on the night of the general meeting and Kiersey shook his hand, congratulating him. What began with some suspicion between Carruthers and Harte turned into a strong and crucial combination.

The two men were quite different: Harte was outgoing whereas Carruthers was reserved. Carruthers, who rarely drank, did not mix as easily with the men as did Harte. They had different approaches in how they dealt with fellow workers, Carruthers tending to take every request or situation seriously whereas Harte was not shy of telling someone where to stuff their petty problem. Both men were highly intelligent and were fond of writing: each of them wrote pieces for WUI periodicals or for Guinness's in-house *Harp* magazine. They also, of course, shared an absolute commitment to trade unionism and the Labour movement.

'It was the surprise of his life that I would work with him and protect him,' Harte recalled of his teaming up with Carruthers. 'I had great respect for him.' They became close friends in their years working together and were exactly the team that union and management needed when tackling their next challenge: Job Evaluation. This would signal another phase of innovative changes in the Brewery.

Seven

O Sole Mio

Work Study and its sequel, Job Evaluation, were part of the march towards modernisation led by Sir Hugh Beaver and championed, in the Dublin brewery, by Sir Charles Harvey. Once upon a time there were employers who told their employees what to do. If the workers did not obey then they were kicked out or locked out. By the time the Workers' Union of Ireland and Guinness had developed their understanding – thanks to the work of Larkin, Harvey, Ferguson, Carruthers, Harte and many others – the prospect of changes in work practices meant the start of a huge phase of negotiations.

Harvey had developed great respect for Larkin and complete trust in the way the trade union functioned in the Brewery. Crucially, the Board of Guinness's also fully trusted Harvey and approved all decisions he made. This combination of elements meant that although the studies, the plans and the negotiations would take years to complete, all was done in a spirit of good will. At times, though, things seemed to be on the brink of collapse into industrial chaos.

Guinness needed to make radical changes to how the brewery worked. There were three possible approaches: to start from scratch with a 'green field site', to shift production completely to Park Royal or to modernise St James's Gate. The latter was the hardest choice, but the WUI workers preferred it. That decision involved, as Jack Harte put it, 'oceans of work'. Because of the amount of work involved, Guinness management asked Larkin for permission to station the

145

Branch Secretary on site in the Brewery. An office was provided for Carruthers in a 'porta-cabin' in the main yard of the St James's Street brewery.

Things got off to a rocky start. The evaluation team completed their work and the next phase was for proposed changes to be examined and discussed at Board level before being presented to the WUI. This took longer than planned but the WUI were presented, on 6 May 1959, with the agreed 'Recommendations of the Team' draft of the job evaluation study.

There was a 'conference' between the Union and the Board on 27 May to discuss the Union's comments on the Team's recommendations. But there had been some intrigue – on both sides – that spiced up that meeting. New Guinness WUI Chairman Jack Harte was working down at the North Wall, in a section of the Brewery known as 'the extension'. Around this time a man came to him from the Brewery and handed Harte a draft of the recommendations dated 27 April. The man had seen it in the office of Chief Engineer Dresser and noticed that there had been amendments written into it. The difference between the two drafts was in how grades would be structured: the proposal Dresser made was that the highest should become Grade 2 to create room for some possible future need for a new Grade 1. Harte immediately posted this document to James Larkin.

The change of the grading structure was, in fact, a good idea that the Union later accepted. But Larkin was angered by the failure of the management to stick with the agreed procedure that the recommendations would be presented to both sides simultaneously. The meeting began in its usual civil manner and then Larkin, accompanied by Carruthers and Harte, put the 27 April draft on the table in fury. 'We started to shout and holler,' Harte recalled, laughing. 'It was a load of bullshit, but they were caught so off guard that they gave a lot of ground on the gradings.'

In a report to Larkin following this meeting, Carruthers wrote:

> I am of the opinion that after completing the job description the Team should have consulted with us on the Factors they were using in comparing one job with another and the points value attached to each. Since they failed to do so, we do not, at the moment, know what method was used in the evaluating of one job as against

another, and since their final proposals contain many anomalies, we must look on the whole thing as suspect.

There was a further union/management meeting in June, this time with Larkin, Carruthers and Harte sitting opposite Harvey and Chamney and, among others, a Mr Atkinson who was a representative of the Job Evaluation firm Ulrick and Orr. Carruthers' summary of the meeting, drawn from minutes taken for the WUI by P. Seery, add some very enjoyable colour to the report of the event.

Larkin expressed the view that there was ill-feeling among the WUI Committee and members towards Job Evaluation and the Panel: 'It was not our fault that this ill feeling existed but it was the Panel's for their handling of the whole business with regard to the disputed documents.' Harvey promised that there were no other hidden documents and it was agreed that the 'final report' of the Panel would be taken as the working basis for the new resident (Permanent) Panel – on which a WUI representative would sit. The Brewery agreed to pay for the training of the selected representative in England.

Larkin then insisted that the WUI must be allowed to check the work of the Panel and how they arrived at the points given. Harvey offered the compromise that Larkin and Carruthers could be given the points system in its entirety but they would not be generally released. Larkin then proposed that the grading structure be reversed: starting at Grade 1 as the lowest level and thus being open to rise as new grades might be added. Harvey agreed with this, but Chamney, the Labour Manager, said it 'would create great administrative difficulties for him'. Harvey was plainly keen to regain the trust and favour of the Union: when Chamney mentioned that another flaw in this changed system was the possibility that a non-tradesman could somehow in the future arrive at a grade that paid more than the wage of a foreman, Larkin said that the Union could accept no such ceiling for its members – and Harvey agreed.

Just as Harte recalled of the time, management had been caught on the hop and Harvey was conceding point after point. Then Larkin went for the financial kill and set out what the Branch Committee's 'considered opinion' was of the value of the new grading structure. The WUI estimated that the cost per year to the Company for this new wage scale would be twenty thousand pounds. As Carruthers quipped in his summary of the meeting: 'In reply Sir Charles, when he had recovered sufficiently, said that it was a very high figure to add to the wages bill annually and added some adjectives to support his view. However, he would refer the matter to his Board for their consideration and would let us have their reply before our next meeting on Tuesday.' Larkin's response to this was to point out that if the Brewery were prepared to spend thousands on new technologies, why would they not spend as much on job evaluation?

Carruthers concluded his summary stating: 'As this is not a verbatim report I have not included, in extenso, the usual 'asides' or verbal skirmishes common to conferences of this nature, as they were important only to the extent that they contributed to our arriving at the present state as incorporated in this report.'

Arthur Guinness Son and Co Ltd reached the grand age of two hundred years old in 1959. A preliminary celebration was held in the Park Royal headquarters but the main celebration was held at St James's Gate on 11 July 1959 with everything from a banquet held at the Rupert Guinness Hall, to music and dance, to a votive Mass held in the parish church near the Brewery. Even the Irish postal service issued a celebratory stamp for Guinness.

In the same week, Jack Carruthers headed a general meeting of the WUI Guinness members to explain developments on the Job Evaluation front and its history. Carruthers told the men that job evaluation made a detailed examination of the job of every worker in the Brewery. The job was observed and analysed and a report written with the headings; 'job description', 'general description', 'where done', 'immediate supervisor', 'controlled by', 'physical tasks', 'mental and clerical tasks', 'cleaning and maintenance', 'responsibility' and 'notes'. On the basis of all this, the worker would be graded and the grading would eventually decide where he fit into the Brewery's pay scale.

As Carruthers summed up:

> Disappointment has been expressed with the value of the declared differentials or grades, but this may be the result of wrongly assuming that the primary function of Job Evaluation was to raise all round the value of the various grades, whereas the real function of Job Evaluation is to see that workers are correctly placed on a grade reflecting the proper value of the jobs they are doing, on a basis of comparison with jobs within the Brewery.

Following Carruthers, Larkin then addressed the workers. He explained the rates of pay that had been negotiated for the new grades and also the task that lay ahead: establishing which grade each worker's job belonged to. The meeting concluded with a substantial majority voting for the proposal: 'The meeting be adjourned and a decision on Job Evaluation be deferred until all jobs were satisfactorily graded.'

When informed by Larkin of the general meeting's decision, Harvey expressed little hope for further negotiation:

> Considering that 1,094 men are due to receive an increase of pay while no man is to drop below his existing wage, I am indeed astonished that the proposals of the Job Evaluation Panel were not accepted, more especially as the Branch Committee and you yourself had recommended acceptance.
>
> If you consider that another discussion with me will be of use I shall, of course, be only too glad to meet you. I must, however, point out, as I have done before, that the Board have agreed to accept the Job Evaluation Panel's recommendations, and in cases where the Panel has not recommended upgrading, the Board has no intention of altering their decision.

Both sides knew that compromise, Ferguson's 'horse trading', was the name of the game. As a result of the Job Evaluation there were 34 jobs 'to be re-described or re-evaluated' and 79 jobs for which the new grading was disputed. Following a further meeting between Larkin and Harvey, the Brewery proposed that if the Panel's recommendations were accepted then those 113 jobs could be re-examined by the Panel. When this proposal was put to a vote by the workers it was narrowly defeated (736 for, 820 against with 12 spoiled votes). The stalemate continued, but now other ploys were tried: just as the union could block implementation of the Job Evaluation, management could highlight problems caused by that decision. Men in the Cleansing Bank of the Cooperage Department and Floorsmen at the Cooke's Lane Maltings, for instance, were due to be upgraded but Personnel Manager Chamney informed Larkin that this could not be done as the intention had been for the Job Evaluation Panel to grade them and they could not do so in the absence of union agreement.

Harvey was trying to break through the stalemate and wrote to Larkin urging a new 'consultative machinery' of departmental and inter-departmental communication between management, union and workers when the matter of new work practices or equipment arose: 'Though ultimate decisions must rest with Management, it is agreed that whenever changes are contemplated, which will affect Labour or existing methods of work, it is important that adequate information should be given to the Union representatives sufficiently early to enable them to consider possible consequences, and make known to Management the views of their members.'

The matter became more drawn-out. At a further general meeting it was decided that rather than taking a vote on new compromises from management the workers would instead initiate a round of discussions within sections of the Brewery. It was a fascinating change of perspective from the workers: even though there were considerable gains on the table for many of them, they still wanted – much to the management's frustration – to debate the matter thoroughly. More changes were made and the Brewery also raised the pay increases that would come with the regrading.

In November 1959 there was yet another heated general meeting: with so much discussion about changes and pay increases, emotions and expectations were running very high. Jack Harte recalled the night vividly: 'We used to have big meetings. Particularly if it was about money. Some of the fellas would come out of the Brewery half-pissed and go into the pub before the meeting.'

It was time to decide on the Job Evaluation process, a meeting due with management the following day having been described by Harvey as probably the last time the matter could be considered. Jack Harte said: 'We were down in the Metropole Hall in Abbey Street with over 1,000 people. Some of them were drunk. Everyone was waiting for the results and the money attached to the results. Jack was trying to read out all the information. All the groups in Guinness's were dealt with separately and Jack had the job of dealing with them all.

'At this meeting, the fellas were fighting for the microphone while Jack was trying to read out the results and I was trying to chair the meeting. Jack was pleading with me to call for order. One man had been tipped off that he was going to get a pay increase and was waiting for this to be announced. He saw another man headed for the microphone and put his foot out to trip him up. A fight broke out between the two of them, struggling on the floor for the microphone. Young Jim Larkin was sitting there watching this and had never seen anything like it.

'One brewery character, George, was pissed out of his mind and had fallen asleep. Amid all the chaos he woke and stood up and started singing 'O Sole Mio'. The odd thing is that the whole meeting changed and came to order. Jack had a terrible night that night, but he handled it well.'

The following day Larkin, Carruthers and Harte met Harvey and his team. Compromise was finally in sight: a few minor alterations were made and a circular issued by the Union to the men ahead of a final ballot vote on the matter. There was a vote in favour of the proposals and so the Job Evaluation system came into effect.

With that huge achievement behind them, so began the real work for Harte and Carruthers: looking for ways of establishing and upgrading the skills of all the general workers represented by the WUI in the Brewery. This sometimes would involve not only skill but a fair amount of imagination.

Harte said that the craft unions started to resent Carruthers because he was having so much success in improving the pay and working conditions of the non-craft workers he represented. Indeed, in an effort to strengthen their position the trade shop stewards formed their own joint alliance: shades of a 'house association'. Interestingly, management consulted James Larkin to ensure that he had no objection to the new council's official recognition and he simply noted a few minor points of protocol. Larkin was also approached by a group of Grade 1 foremen seeking to join the WUI but was obliged to tell them that under the agreed conditions of the Union when given full negotiation rights by the Brewery that grade was specifically excluded.

But the launch of the regrading brought conflict and tension to the factory floor. There were divisive intrigues going on and some men were criticising the Union while not being willing to get involved themselves in the work needed in this mammoth task. Funnily enough, one of the men Harte recalled as guilty of being a hurler on the ditch was Tommy Garry – who would later not only become an active trade unionist but even rose to General President of the WUI and General Secretary of SIPTU. As Harte put it: 'this alleged hurler on the ditch proved to be no slouch and I am indebted to him for his help and our friendship that lives on.' Another of these men was Larry Doyle – and he also later became an active trade unionist and became General Secretary of the Mechanical Engineers' Union! Jack Harte felt impelled to write an open letter in December 1959 attacking 'self-seeking individuals':

> We, as the democratically elected ruling body of your Branch, are very perturbed by the fact that the ludicrous position of Department watching Department and man against man should show itself at this particular time when a united front is called for now more than ever, especially when it appears that the Company's progressive drive is about to be intensified. We are at a loss to understand whether the culprits are frustrated as to their own failure to gain favour for lucrative posts, or could it be the type who continually refuses to accept responsibility as a representative despite repeated nominations. Should the guilty parties fit either category I say to them, 'You have no right to exploit your fellow creatures by introducing specious fallacies in such a way as to dominate a man's thinking.' Based on emotional and psychological

factors speculation can be very dangerous to our future dealings with Management. Therefore I urge you to co-operate with your Branch Officers in stamping out this pattern of muddled reasoning, and leave the problems in the hands of men whom you elected for their integrity and wide experience.

. . .

Finally, let me say, don't be a sucker for the shop floor orator, the barrack room lawyer or the back bench heckler who rarely shows his true form openly. Bear in mind that if someone expresses views they are merely his opinion and not the opinion of the General Body.

It was plainly the case with money and promotion in the air that there were dissident voices. As Jack Carruthers had written on another occasion, it should be a matter of sticking with the WUI motto 'each for all' and not 'every man for himself'. During this intense time Harte would often write such open letters to be circulated. But there was even sabotage in the air: he recalled that the bundles of circulars were often spotted floating down the Liffey!

As 1960 began, the practical work of the Job Evaluation Panel was set to begin. Two members of the trade union were to be trained up to take part in the process and the deliberations. Larkin sent his annual letter to Harvey seeking, this time, a raise of ten shillings a week for his members. Harvey was completely against this. In his response, he noted that the Brewery's profits had fallen by £161,000 in 1959 and yet the men had been given 'the same Christmas and Prosperity bonuses as in the previous year'. He wrote: 'These bonuses represented an average per head per week of one pound, nine shillings and sixpence. They certainly could be regarded as peculiar to Guinness!'

Harvey said the Board could offer an increase of three shillings and Larkin said that he could not possibly go back to the men with such a low offer. Harvey and the Board drew the line at five shillings a week and this was accepted by the general membership at a meeting. Perhaps horse trading was, indeed, catching on.

Jack Carruthers, giving his report on 1959 at the annual general meeting early in 1960, looked back on that year saying 'Last year has been one of continuous dispute with Management, on almost everything under the sun, but the major ones in connection with Job Evaluation and promotion'. He reminded those present of the importance of trade unionism:

> I can say without fear of contradiction, that had we not got the powerful organisation we have today, many of our present members, including myself, would have been forced through Brewery economic measures to join the emigrant ship. Despite the worldwide ballyhoo concerning the Brewery, I have long found that sentiment has little influence on the application of these economic measures where they affect our workers' interests. Remember this, friends, that there is ultimately only one power that any Management recognises and respects and that is the power of organised labour. If we cannot protect ourselves by discussion across the conference table, then we must be prepared to fight. Peace and good labour relations are our sincere objective, but if the price we must pay is servility to our Masters, then honour decrees that we reject those terms.

It was a view that set the tone for what lay ahead in perhaps the Brewery's most troublesome year since the Workers' Union of Ireland first made its presence felt at Guinness's. No sooner was the Job Evaluation Panel to be launched than the whole process started to unravel. Larkin informed Harvey that the Branch Committee wanted the shop stewards to go through the research done by the job evaluation team to see how they came up with their grading decisions. This would also, he said, 'have a profound psychological effect in demonstrating to the men that there was nothing concealed or underhand in the working of Job Evaluation'. Harvey replied, complaining: 'Mr Chamney tells me that the situation at the moment is rapidly becoming impossible in that the Shop Stewards seem to consider it is up to them to query and argue about every assessment – no doubt they are pressed to do so by the men they represent'. Harvey decided that once the chosen trade union representatives for the Panel were trained up they would have access to whatever documentation they wanted, but the Company would not agree to having the research openly available. Larkin and the Branch rejected this and so there was yet a new stumbling block to the proposed changes. It was as if the WUI were finally waking up to the full implications of job evaluation for the workers they represented. Carruthers, infuriated by Harvey's response and Chamney's comments, wrote:

> No Shop Steward queries any assessment without my sanction and we have been most careful in allowing only legitimate complaints to go forward.
>
> As a matter of record of recent date we only challenged about three of the Panel's findings and in all three we sustained our case. If raising these cases constituted an "impossible situation" then Mr Chamney can expect to be perpetually involved. At a recent meeting with Mr Chamney and Mr Leeson, we made it quite clear that we did not accept the former's contention that the Panel, being "experts" were infallible and must not be challenged. We then, in the course of the argument established that though the job in dispute had been accurately described, the Panel had not attached sufficient significance to some of the items constituting the job and undertook to re-examine them in the light of our argument. So much for Mr Chamney's "experts".

Jack Carruthers, one-time amateur boxer, was, after seven years in his job as Branch Secretary, squaring up for the defining fight of his career. Within months, as troubles in the Brewery escalated, he would have a direct showdown with Harvey.

In his family memoir, Jack Carruthers wrote about a strategy he encouraged the Union to adapt for bringing change to union/management relations:

> I argued against wasting time having a go at foremen or junior clerks and convinced them that if the managers could be frightened and broken then the domino effect would bring down the whole rotten system. And that is what happened. They asked me how did one break so powerful a personage with a century of tradition supporting him? I told them the answer was quite simple, based on the psyche of each human being. First and foremost, a manager was also an employee, with all the ambitions of any brewery employee, and his was twofold. Firstly, a social one, as providing he was acceptable to the Board, i.e. the Guinness family, he was invited to their Garden Parties and was acceptable socially to them.
>
> This situation could be maintained if those he was responsible for were not a source of embarrassment to the Board.

I achieved my objective, as the managers realised their own vulnerability and that we represented a serious impediment to their social and employment ambitions. To protect themselves, they issued instructions down the line that Union trouble was not to reach their level. Their immediate subordinate in turn, to protect their interests issued instructions to the foremen to settle disputes and not embarrass them!! And they, the last line of defence, who all their working lives had received the unqualified support of top management, did not know how to cope with this new and frightening situation.

A perfect example of Carruthers' strategy was demonstrated through his handling of problems for 'lads' employed in the Bottling Plant. The foremen were pushing the lads too hard and, in Carruthers' opinion, even abusing their health while always reminding them of the threat that, by brewery rules, when a lad reached the age of twenty-one he had no promise of continued employment. The foremen were doing this in response to their own immediate supervisor, a Mr Shanaghan. Carruthers went to the top – to Mr J. C. P. Anderson, Brewer in charge of By-Products – outlining the strains between the employees and the foremen in this section. In his very polite letter to Anderson following their meeting he wrote:

When a reason for this action of the Foremen was sought it was suggested that they adopted this course through fear of leaving themselves open to criticism by Mr Shanaghan with whom they sometimes had personal differences. This may or may not be true, but if it is so it is a ridiculous position to maintain and is wrong if the lads suspect discord between Management and Foremen.

You will agree that it is not conductive to good relations, so necessary in modern industry, if it is evident that instead of mutual trust and respect, an atmosphere of mistrust and fear prevails.

We feel that your serious consideration of the points raised here will result in your being able to restore an atmosphere of mutual trust and respect which in turn leads to a relaxation of the ever present tensions of industrial life. The Rapier, with its renowned flexibility, will not snap as easily as the rigid sword!

The pride of place of the St James's Gate brewery was, meanwhile, being eroded. In 1959 Guinness started advertising its product in Ireland for the first time – up to then, the pint had been so popular, holding at least three-quarters of the market, that advertising was unnecessary. But then a more extraordinary move was made by the company: a new brewery with a new product. The market for lagers and ales had been growing over the decades and Guinness decided it was finally time to come up with a product for those drinkers. Guinness hired the German master brewer Doctor Herman Münder to create a lager for them. He was brought to Ireland and the Company decided not to base work from St James's Gate but instead they acquired the Great Northern Brewery in Dundalk as the site for the lager's production. In choosing the name for their new product they simply went for the name of their own Guinness logo: and so Harp Lager was born. It was first released in bottle form only and a few years later it was released in draught. The pint of plain now had competition from its own brewers.

And industrial relations in St James's Gate were in a downward spiral. There were several disputes going on at the same time – about the above-mentioned treatment of 'lads' in the Bottling Plant, about promotions in the Power House, about grading and regrading in various sections including the Gate Porters and the Barley Kiln Stokers. Agreement on union access to all Job Evaluation Panel documentation was also still not in sight. On this issue, Harvey offered the Union a range of options including bringing the head of the Park Royal Job Evaluation Panel over to discuss the situation with the Branch Committee.

The situation in the Power House escalated at the end of May, at which time James Larkin was out of the country on a long trip first to attend the annual conference of the International Labour Organisation in Geneva and then to take a holiday in London. This meant that Jack Carruthers, as next in command in the union brewery situation, dealt directly with Sir Charles Harvey. It was the old grievance of senior men being passed over for promotion, and the WUI men in the section had decided to take strike action if the senior man, Grogan, was not promoted. Harvey had already written a detailed justification for Grogan's not being selected, but this was still rejected by the men and Carruthers wrote to him on 7 June saying the men would begin a series of stoppages starting 15 June.

The month of James Larkin's absence turned into a nerve-racking time for Jack Carruthers. The men in the Power House voted for an all-out strike and at the same time Carruthers' Branch Committee was pressing him to put forward a resolution to the Board demanding: 'No new machines or methods be introduced resulting from Work Study until a fully comprehensive agreement is concluded between the Board and the Workers' Union of Ireland. This agreement is to cover, firstly, our right to work and secondly, a proper share in the profits.' Carruthers did not forward this resolution to the Board, feeling that to do so would be to renege on agreements already made between union and management, and he was censured by the Committee. He wrote to Denis Larkin, younger brother of James and at that time Industrial Secretary of the WUI, informing him of the resolution and its background and also of the vote to strike in the Power Station. The entire Brewery was about to shut down as the men acted in solidarity with one worker who had been passed over for the rather humble promotion from Grade 5 to Grade 4.

As the due date for a general strike loomed, there was a coincidental visit from London of Lord Iveagh and Sir Hugh Beaver. When Harvey informed them of the situation all met with the full Board and the decision was finally made to change the promotion policy in the company: if a manager decided not to promote the senior man then that man had to be given a week's notice of this so he had the option of going to the union to seek representation on the issue. To avoid the strike, the Board also decided to backdate the decision and grant Grogan his promotion as he had been denied its benefit of shop steward intercession. His promotion was also backdated six months to when it should have happened.

The men in the Power House agreed to this offer and the strike threat was called off. But this was more than a matter of a crisis being averted. Another pillar of the old ways had fallen: the union now had a say in the promotion process in the Brewery. Jack Carruthers had finally won the breakthrough he had been seeking for almost a decade. Management later made the further concession that if they and the Union could not agree on a particular case of a man being passed over for promotion then both sides could go to an outside third party – most likely the Labour Court or someone recommended by that body – for adjudication.

When Harvey and Larkin met again in July, with the Power House strike threat behind them but still with much unrest in the Brewery, Larkin again went over the litany of problems being created by the pace of modernisation. After deliberating on this with the Board, Harvey wrote to Larkin with a conciliatory gesture that they had:

> . . . instructed our Managers to go slow over introducing new methods the main effect of which would be to reduce labour. They should concentrate rather on methods which would improve productivity and reduce waste. The new Surplus Yeast Plant is a case in point.
>
> The Work Study Department have been given similar instructions and they are now concentrating mainly on reducing clerical work and paper, while at the same time being responsible for examining all new projects to ensure that their layout combines maximum efficiency with minimum fatigue to the operators. Here the new Tank Filling Station is an example.

Harvey made a further concession to cool the unrest. He ended the management's side of the stalemate by saying that jobs due for regrading could proceed, without prejudice to any final decision made by the Job Evaluation Panel, so that men who were overdue promotion and pay increase could have them. Meanwhile, in October, William Gibson and Patrick Bolger were selected as the trade union representatives to be trained in Bristol for a place on the Permanent Job Evaluation Panel.

But then, in November, Sir Charles Harvey led the final breakthrough to end the impasse. Just as years before, when he had given the Works Committee one last chance as a functioning method of conducting union/management negotiations and then abandoned it, he again took decisive and crucial action.

After further discussions with Larkin, Harvey sent him a draft of a letter he proposed writing to him as a matter of record with the aim of taking all contentious issues out of job evaluation. With Larkin's suggestions incorporated, Harvey sent the letter from Guinness to the WUI. It began:

> It has become increasingly evident in recent months that the present system of Job Evaluation, as applied at St James's Gate, does not give results which satisfy management and the Workers' Union of Ireland in all cases. During their recent visit to Bristol, members of the Job Evaluation Panel and Workers' Union of Ireland representatives were given details of other systems of Job Evaluation, and they have suggested that it should be possible to produce a system more suited to our needs in the Brewery.

He went on to outline how the decks would be cleared of any issues that had created this stalemate: a broader-based union and management advisory committee would be set up to establish a new version of job evaluation; in the meantime all 113 disputed jobs, plus new jobs that had evolved, would be judged by union and management together and their decision submitted to the Board; retrospective pay would apply to upgrades in these categories to catch up with the raises granted to the workers already upgraded. As Harvey concluded in his letter: 'It is hoped that this scheme will prove acceptable to your members, and will be a means whereby all the doubts and uncertainties created in their minds by Job Evaluation may be finally dissipated, thus enabling a new start to be made with Job Evaluation, with the agreement and active participation of the Workers' Union of Ireland'.

Larkin's reply, after the Branch Committee had discussed Harvey's proposal, was basically positive but noted that it would help ease the tensions that had built up if 'all present claims be conceded where there is a responsible basis for the claim, and the claim is endorsed by the Chief Shop Steward and Branch Officers'.

It's interesting to note, in the midst of all this, that the relationship between the Union and Harvey was becoming ever more friendly. At the end of 1960 Jack Carruthers sent his Christmas greetings to Harvey on behalf of the Union and the Branch Committee. Harvey sent a handwritten note back to him: 'Thank you and the Brewery Branch Committee very much for your good wishes, which I cordially reciprocate. 1960 has not been an easy year for any of us, and I fully realise your difficulties have been greater than mine. I sincerely hope that 1961 will see us with a clearer and happier atmosphere from all points of view.'

Jack Harte recalled that Carruthers and Harvey developed a mutual admiration and fondness. Harvey, living across from the Brewery gates and with his offices inside, was often seen taking his red setter dogs for a walk in the area. If he saw Carruthers out and about he would raise his walking stick and call out "hey ho, Carruthers!"

The situation, at one stage on the brink of drastic conflict, calmed down. By March 1961, after much correspondence and many meetings, the official and agreed 'List of Jobs in Settlement, showing changes of Grade and retrospective Dates' was issued. The Board had conceded on every claim made by the Union. Everyone on the list was upgraded at least one notch. Many had their upgrade retrospective all the way back more than a year to September 1959 when the other upgrades had been set. It was a huge triumph for the workers who had been so beleaguered with the changes and redundancies sweeping through the Brewery in the previous years. Larkin wrote to Harvey to tell him that the proposal had been accepted at a general meeting: 'I may state that the vote was most representative, the number of votes cast being the greatest in the history of the Guinness Branch and the decision for acceptance was supported by a majority vote in excess of 70 percent.' Larkin concluded by writing: 'Finally, I desire to convey to you personally an appreciation of the manner in which you have earnestly sought to provide the basis of an acceptable solution of the many problems which have faced us during the past few months.'

The Job Evaluation Advisory Committee consisted of the five men who had been sent to Bristol for training (including WUI men Bolger and Gibson). They set to work, their aim being to produce a report that would propose a new job evaluation system. They would consult with all levels and departments in the Brewery.

This report was ultimately finalised and agreed in July 1962. It meticulously set out the purpose and principles of job evaluation. It set out the agreed 'factors' in a job (defined in the report as 'the basic kinds of human abilities and endurances that are required by all jobs, but in different quantities and qualities') and how agreement was reached on measuring these. Sixty-one jobs had been selected as an agreed cross-section of work in the Brewery and these had been analysed in depth. The report also applied a new term for the non-skilled workers: 'operatives'. In presenting the new system of job evaluation, the aspects to be considered were: 'skill' – measured by the length of time required to learn the job; 'discretion' – measured by the degree of autonomy with which the operative worked; 'physical effort' – ranging from light to heavy physical work; 'job conditions' – measuring any environmental hardships involved in the job; 'hazard' – measuring risk of injury on the job; 'safety of others' – measuring the level of carefulness required to prevent injury to others. This could all be presented in chart form. It was a far more comprehensive approach than had been taken in the initial Job Evaluation.

By the time the report was launched, however, one of the key players in the great changes that had happened in industrial relations in the Brewery in the previous fifteen years had left the stage.

Eight

Changes at the Helm

Relations between the workers and management in the Brewery had been transformed. Workers discovered they had a voice, management discovered they had ears. Instead of drawing battle lines, employers could safely dare to communicate with those who were needed at every level to keep on providing the product that turned the wheels of their relative wealth: the perfect pint. Job evaluation was the dissecting of every small measure of how a man at the lowest grade did work that created wealth for some shareholder at the 'highest' level. The walls not only of class but of class consciousness had fallen down. It was equal rights for all voices. The working man could define his reward for the work he provided to his employer. Harvey had been the key management figure in accepting this change. Instead of digging in his heels he went with the flow. He transformed the working structure of the Guinness brewery.

With this huge task complete, seventy-three-year-old Sir Charles Offley Harvey decided it was time to retire. He had become very popular with the workers and he had been a truly inspirational leader, encouraging everything from sports to cultural activity in the Brewery. He had also co-founded the Irish Management Institute and had been its head for several years. A lesser man would have railed against the changes needed to bring industrial relations in the Brewery into the twentieth century, or simply have ignored it and sat back in his office by the fire reading the newspaper. His lively mind and his wish to understand those he led were hallmarks of greatness. That he and his wife were respectively presidents of the Men's and the Ladies' Guinness Golfing Societies was just one example of many aspects to their social involvement with brewery life.

A special feature about Harvey in the Guinness in-house magazine *Harp* on the occasion of his retirement included a poem about the man by none other than Jack Harte. The last verses were:

> Had not this man
> Come on the scene
> I doubt if we could have seen
> An era that was fought so clean.
>
> Despite his overwhelming size
> His humble heart could compromise
> 'Twas awkward for to try and fight
> A decent man
>
> Who had such height.
> The word that he would give to you
> Rang out as sound as Guinness Brew
> No man can say that he once welshed
> No one can say he used his bench
> But rather that he set aside
> The line that our ranks divide.
>
> Sir Charles, now you are on your way
> To rest from work – and have some play
> We wish you happy days galore
> Amid your kin on another shore.
>
> And as your troubles they grow thin
> I think of what they might have been
> If you had not by words and deeds
> Set the example for all creeds.

Larkin wrote a farewell letter to Harvey that is so remarkable it merits being quoted in full:

> Dear Sir Charles,
>
> Although I may see you again before you officially sever your connection with the Brewery, there is always the possibility that we might not meet again.

Because of that I feel I should write you this personal letter.

Although we have appeared on opposite and probably opposing sides, and while we may disagree on many matters, I have a very high personal regard for you and the special qualities you have displayed while representing the Brewery in our many encounters.

The period since 1949, when our trade union first entered on the Brewery scene, has been a testing one: a test for the Board; a test for the workers. That the outcome has been good and that a reasonable relationship has been established between the Board, Management and Union is, in my opinion, almost solely due to you. It is a pity, possibly, that our most recent major issue, the 40 hour week, continues as a source of friction at the point of your departure. We all like to think we have tied up all the loose ends.

I think you can take pride in a considerable personal achievement over the past twelve years. Without your presence, I think there could well have been, on several occasions, a major and bitter conflict, which would leave its scars behind for many years.

It must be some satisfaction to you, as one of the persons mainly responsible for establishing the Institute of Management, that in your own sphere of responsibility you have given an outstanding example of how to treat men as human beings and how to establish industrial relations on a basis of mutual trust and respect, even though the issues be sharp and the methods used somewhat extreme at times.

I wish you well in your well-earned years of retirement. May they be many; may they continue to be fruitful in achievement; may they be peaceful and enriched with the contentment of many jobs well done.

Harvey wrote back, thanking Larkin for the letter and the wishes expressed, but also not missing an opportunity for a little jibe:

I do not in the least regret having been largely instrumental in bringing the Brewery within the folds of the Trade Union. It was a natural course and it would have done nobody any good had we tried to resist your entrance.

I have always held the opinion that while the Union must at times oppose management, it is equally important that they should co-operate with management for the general good of the firm and all its employees. I think you have taken the same view and I have always found you most reasonable to deal with, though at times perhaps I have thought you were inclined to let your children run on too loose a rein! However, you in your wisdom probably knew better, and I am very glad to think that during the twelve years you and I have been associated we have managed to avoid any serious trouble. Long may this continue and I am sure you will be equally helpful and understanding to my successor.

Sir Charles was a hard act to follow. Into Harvey's place – even into his one-time home of 98 St. James's Street – came Sir Geoffrey Thompson. Again, a knighted ex-military man. In his thirty-six-year military career he had served as Staff Officer under General Eisenhower in the Mediterranean region and had won a Distinguished Service Order as commander of the field artillery in Italy. In the years after the war he became Chief of Staff at Anti-Aircraft Command and later Commander of the Number Two Army Group Royal Artillery in Egypt. By the time he retired from the army in 1961 he had become Military Secretary: a post making him responsible for policies on personnel management in the British Army. This might not have been a good preparation for the task he faced in the radically changed Guinness brewery. A profile of Thompson in Guinness's *Harp* magazine described him as a shy man who enjoyed hunting and fishing. Unlike Harvey, he did not enjoy team sports. He had also joined the Kildare Hunt, a fox-hunting club. Thompson and his wife – who served in the Women's Auxiliary Air Force during World War Two – had one adult daughter living in the United States.

The changes in Dublin were mirrored in Park Royal. Sir Hugh Beaver, who had suffered a heart attack in the late 1950s, retired at the end of late 1960 at the age of seventy. He was replaced by Lord Alan Lennox-Boyd, titled Viscount Boyd of Merton in the House of Lords. Boyd was a Conservative politician who had served as Minister and had also been Secretary of State for the Colonies. Though his politics were right wing, he was reportedly a very affable man – he was also, like Harvey, very tall: six foot five. But now there were two old-school men dealing with the new, confident trade union in the Dublin brewery.

Harte recalled that Thompson was very different from Harvey: Harte's impression was that Thompson thought Harvey had yielded too much to the WUI and wanted to stand firmer. There were residual issues from the whole Job Evaluation process: men who had not been given the increases they felt they deserved. A set of jobs in the Brewhouse – 'by-products' (which included returned sub-standard Guinness), Bottling Plant and Hop Stores – were grouped together by Jack Carruthers in an attempt to strengthen their case. There had already been problems with the manager of this Department and Carruthers, who had accused him in writing of 'thumbing his nose at all sections under his jurisdiction', was trying to use this grouping tactically as a way to win better conditions for these men.

In the last weeks of Harvey's tenure, with no progress being made on this case, Carruthers received permission from Larkin and the General Executive Committee to initiate a series of one-hour stoppages in the Brewhouse. Still there was no progress. Jack Harte was with Carruthers at a meeting with Thompson not long after Harvey's retirement. Carruthers was presenting his case for these men, but Thompson refused to change the gradings. Carruthers was always looking for ways to increase the pay packet for the union members but now he had strayed onto thin ice: he simply did not have a convincing case for these men. He had to bring Larkin in to support the case for these upgrades – but a further problem was that Larkin didn't agree with Carruthers' argument, either. The issue, however, had become something of a power struggle between the Union and the Brewery's new boss so Larkin had to press the case. Thompson still refused. After the meeting, Larkin turned to Carruthers when they left the Board room and said 'don't ever put me in a situation like that again.'

But by now the whole matter had escalated: Carruthers needed to win this battle, but he had chosen a very weak test case for his first engagement with Thompson. Harte came to the rescue, seeing that the only way forward was to take a gamble. He suggested that they issue a flyer, to be distributed throughout the Brewery by the shop stewards, decrying how inflexible management were being. A general meeting was called and the men now rallied around Carruthers' bid to get an upgrade for the group he was trying to help. The weight of numbers so firmly on his side, Carruthers went back to Thompson who agreed to do a re-evaluation of the group: they got their wage increase. It was a victory for the WUI – but this was only a battle and the real war had yet to begin.

Around this time, also, there was an incident that would have been unimaginable in the early days when even Harvey said that non-skilled workers should not attend meetings between trade union officials and Board members. Carruthers and Harte were meeting members of the Board and one of them, who had just come back from America, said to Carruthers 'So you're the mouthpiece.'

As Harte put it, Carruthers gave the man 'a tongue lashing', saying: 'I have not had the benefit of your sojourn in America, but I am the Branch Secretary of the Number Nine Branch of the Workers' Union of Ireland,' and then launched into a tirade against the man's disrespect for trade unionism.

From the days of trade unionism for the non-skilled workers in the Brewery being resisted, to the day when being a member of a trade union was a condition of employment; from the days when there were rules of employment in the Brewery that employees were not allowed to read, to the day when Harvey invited the union to help him come up with a system for evaluating their work; from the days of Harvey requesting that non-skilled workers not be brought to union/management meetings; to the day when a man who had been a sawyer in the Cooperage Department could tell off a member of the Guinness Board of Directors for impudence. Guinness's had come a long way indeed.

Steps towards another trade union milestone – the five-day forty-hour working week – had been taken in the final months of Sir Charles Harvey's tenure, but the Board (to Harvey's own expressed regret in a letter to Larkin) did not concede because it felt more study had to be done into how output could be rescheduled to facilitate such a change. As the months rolled by, this led to some tension between Larkin and Carruthers: wages in Ireland were on the rise again, catching up with the rising cost of living. Carruthers and his Branch Committee wanted Larkin to press the Brewery for a wage increase but Larkin felt this was bad policy: seeking a wage increase and a shorter working week at the same time gave management the opportunity to play both proposals off each other.

Finally, in October 1961, the Board of Directors offered a 41 ¼-hour five-day week. They also promised to try reducing Saturday work as much as possible and paying time-and-a-third for Saturday work. But there were several provisos in the ever-changing work environment in the Brewery:

> That the company have the right to take full advantage of the most modern methods of working, with full co-operation of the Union in the prosecution and implementation of Work Study and any other means of increasing productivity.
>
> That the company will train employees so that every man shall be trained to do any job in the same grade which is considered desirable that he should relieve.
>
> The right of the Board to institute shifts outside the three traditional shifts now worked should this be considered necessary.

Larkin was in with a pay increase claim even as this agreement was being accepted, and in a further sign of a changed climate the Board came back with an offer far lower than expected: the Union had anticipated perhaps thirty shillings, the offer instead was twenty shillings. Larkin warned, in a letter sent 26 October, that a general meeting was coming up soon and he believed that the men, when told of this offer, would insist on nothing less than thirty shillings. He wrote: 'The Board made a serious error on making such a relatively low initial offer, compared to increases in other employments, and the result will be to cause resentment and growing impatience among the employees.' He went on to list higher pay increases being accepted by several other main employers and gave the usual reminder that the Brewery could easily afford a higher pay increase. Before the general meeting, the Board came back with an offer of a twenty-five shilling increase. It was accepted by the Union membership.

Thompson had established a more reticent approach between the management and the Union. The heady days of giants like Larkin and Harvey engaging first in confrontation and later in co-operation were over. But the growing pace of change in the Brewery in terms of methods of work and production brought more flashpoints of trouble. And Thompson's style, unfortunately, did not make things easier.

The changes brought in by Job Evaluation and Work Study, on the other hand, were breathtaking. A union memo from around this time gives an overview of changes in the previous years. The introduction of an electric lift in the Hop Stores released seven men from duty for nine months of the year. In the Surplus Yeast Collecting Plant, experts had been hired to improve the plant but could not find a way. Then the workers in the plant took an interest in the process and came up with suggestions. The men were awarded sixty-five pounds for their suggestions: the changes yielded a one-thousand-pound saving and a 15 percent increase in output. Elsewhere, the changes brought a 150 percent increase in the amount of yeast processed, with the loss of four jobs. Jobs in the workshops – fitters, boiler-makers and so on – were on average halved. The abolition of barges, using the Irish canal system, saved £24,000 a year and caused forty redundancies. There were huge savings in the Container Department: new sterilising techniques meant a reduction of hops required and total savings were estimated at two hundred and eighty six thousand pounds. Work Study techniques for the reduction in beer wastage led to a saving of ten thousand pounds a year. The change from wooden barrels to metal casks meant a drop from thirty seven to seventeen men in the Cleansing Bank. Six jobs were lost when the narrow-gauge railway was abolished and replaced with the more efficient tractor and trailer system. A 'cipper system' of number taking to keep track of the casks was studied and the realisation made that it was far more economic to lose a percentage of casks than it was to follow the movements of them all. The system was ended with the loss of jobs for all forty 'lads' employed for that task.

A note from the Branch Committee summed up the situation: 'One of our greatest difficulties for years has been our lack of knowledge regarding the actual savings which resulted from the introduction of new methods, systems and machinery. Further to this we have had no means provided to us whereby we could measure the value of our output per head.' Jack Carruthers had already, with funding cleared by Larkin, bought books on Work Study to read and share, and colleagues from other WUI branches had also offered advice on the matter. A National Productivity Committee had been established at the instigation of a number of organisations, including the Irish Management Institute Harvey had co-founded, and so this was becoming the burning topic of the time in the Labour movement.

Early in 1962 the sweep of changes, the Union's concerns for its members and Thompson's managerial style led to their inevitable collision. The O. K. Corral in the Guinness brewery was the Spargers Section.

New equipment and work techniques were ready to be introduced to the Spargers Section (sparging is a process of rinsing the 'wort', or unfermented beer, from the spent grain). The men in the Spargers Section deserved, and had sought, an upgrade for this new work method. Management had offered to upgrade some of the men, and then outlined further tasks they would need to take on. The Spargers rejected this. Thompson wanted to go ahead and introduce the changes ahead of agreement with the men and Larkin wrote to him asking that this be deferred until they had an opportunity to discuss the matter. He added: 'My further purpose in seeking deferment is that for some weeks now we have been seriously engaged in discussion through a special Policy Committee within the Branch on the overall problem of production and the interest of the Company and of the employees thereon and the resultants gains'.

Days later, this Policy Committee proposed the motion: 'That the Branch Committee affirm the principle that benefits from co-operation in productivity measures are the property of all our members and should be shared accordingly with all our members equally'. This committee outlined the changes that were clearly coming nationally and in the way the Brewery worked. It concluded: 'The policy of the Branch Committee so far in productivity techniques has been one of guarded co-operation and by an adroit use of the prior consultation machinery we have fought a reasonably successful rearguard action. The urgent question before us is to make a realistic assessment of the whole situation and realise that reluctant co-operation may no longer suffice. The Policy Committee feel that we have no choice but to fully co-operate, but the obligation is upon the Branch Committee to secure the maximum guarantees and controls in safeguarding existing employment, take home pay, dignity of the worker and to try to maintain conditions which would enable the worker to exercise responsibility and initiative and to share in the benefits of his co-operation in increased productivity'.

Larkin, Carruthers and Harte had a prearranged meeting with Thompson and his team in January about other matters relating to changes in the Brewery. Thompson tried to tag the issue of the Spargers onto the end of the meeting, but Larkin said he would rather have a separate meeting and this was arranged for 2 February. At that meeting the union side again sought to stress the need for broader discussions on productivity and changes in work methods. The Union side offered to bring the Spargers problem down a notch back to the local shop steward so that the broader issues could be discussed at the union/management level. As Harte and Carruthers wrote in their report of this meeting: 'Sir Geoffrey paid no attention to this gesture and showed his determination by standing up before our side had done so. Finally the Branch Secretary warned that trouble would result because of this unwise decision'. The report then noted: 'The gauntlet was thrown down and we accepted the challenge'.

On 6 February 1962 Carruthers and Harte issued a special union notice stating:

> Arising from an emergency meeting of the Branch Committee on 5th February to consider the rejection by the Board of Directors of the very reasonable request to postpone implementing the change in the Spargers Section until the 19th of February, the date on which the Branch Committee would have been prepared to discuss

the whole question of future changes relating to productivity, we now direct all members to work to rule and not to work any overtime as from noon today, TUESDAY 6th of FEBRUARY, until further notice.

On the same day, Carruthers sent a handwritten letter to Larkin explaining the action being taken and telling him the Spargers had also been instructed by the Branch Committee 'not to use the new method implemented by management'. He wrote of the Committee: 'In reviewing the attitude of management during the past few months and taking into account the recent Board rejection of our very reasonable request for postponement of the change, it is their firm conviction that Management are not anxious to sit in partnership on productivity with us, but are content to try and force changes with the ultimate object of greatly reducing the labour content without having to make any further concessions to us through negotiations.'

Larkin received, on the same day, a letter from Thompson with a copy of the union special notice attached. Displaying a very surprising lack of one of the most fundamental tenets of trade unionism, Thompson wrote: 'The instruction by the Brewery Branch of the Union banning overtime in the Brewery as a whole, on account of this one matter of Spargers reorganization does, frankly, seem to me to be unnecessary and provocative.' His defence for the action taken by management was that the new method had been ready for implementation since the previous December and, while he wished to start discussions on 19 February, he wanted to go ahead with this overdue change.

Larkin's response to Thompson was brief and cool: 'If there has been misunderstanding or lack of clear and effective communication between Management and Branch Committee it is regrettable and emphasises the need for general overall discussion of the wide field of increased productivity.' Larkin was willing to meet 'on the 19th instant, or such other date when we may be ready'. He was leaving Thompson to stew in his juices.

Carruthers and Harte, meanwhile, called for a general meeting for 13 February with the agenda 'Report on present situation and decision in respect of STRIKE

ACTION'. On the eve of this meeting Thompson wrote to Larkin, the reality finally dawning on him: 'We seem to be drifting towards a danger of precipitate action which would do great harm to many people.' Cloaking his climb-down behind concerns for the 'trade and livelihood of people who had nothing to do with this quarrel' he wrote:

> I therefore write you this letter to inform you that, while Management firmly intends that the Spargers Section shall be reorganized, the Board is willing to do all that is possible to provide that the reorganisation is carried out in a manner which is mutually acceptable. I am very willing to meet you for further discussion of the handling of this reorganisation. The essential is that people on both sides of this argument, and those who can take no part in it, should not suffer from any harmful action which might have been avoided.

The strike action was called off, the changes in the Spargers Section were called off and everyone took a pause to cool down. Then Larkin displayed a perfect example of how he merited the title of leader for a 'thinking, intelligent movement'. He wrote a six-page densely typed letter to Thompson in which he, basically, gave the new Assistant Managing Director a guide to the importance of consultation. More importantly, he also outlined step-by-step how peace and understanding between both sides could be achieved. Some of what Larkin proposed was based on the report drawn up by the Guinness Branch's Policy Committee.

Larkin set out the context of workers' concerns about productivity, recognising that they needed to develop a more positive attitude about this. He also acknowledged the pressure on the management side in a more competitive market with changing tastes. Of concern for all was the possibility of Ireland's joining the Common Market (precursor to the European Union) and what effect that might have on the nation's economy. Larkin said that the peaceful unionisation of Guinness since 1949 was a credit to both sides. The new challenges since 1957 and the introduction of Work Study and Job Evaluation had been accepted by the trade union and its members, but the extent and effect of the changes was causing problems. He wrote:

If there is to be a common and co-operative approach to the problem of increasing productivity, then it can only be on the basis of equal opportunities to participate in the study of the problem.

To that end we first envisage the establishment of a Joint Productivity Committee, based on complete integrity on each side.

Secondly, to ensure the willing and intelligent participation of the general body of the members of the Union in support of the Joint Productivity Committee and its efforts to increase productivity, certain guarantees will require to be given by the Board in respect of the security of employment and conditions of work of our members.

Thirdly, that there shall be a clear and well-defined scheme under which our members receive a fair and reasonable share of the gains which may flow from increasing productivity.

Larkin gave a detailed proposal of exactly how this Committee would be composed – with representatives from every level from top to bottom in the Brewery – and how often it would meet. The Committee would receive from management, annually, a three-year report on forecasts of finance and productivity. Detailing more about how this system would work, Larkin was actually laying down a manifesto for the Brewery by which its old hierarchical structure would be gone for once and for all and every level would have an equal voice: a template for a radically progressive company. He also set out the agenda for finally winning long-sought concessions: that Christmas and Prosperity annual bonuses be guaranteed; that a formula be found to link those bonuses to company profits; that individual workers be paid a share of the profits from their increased productivity; that the threat of lay-off for boys when they finished their term be removed so that they automatically continued work as men in the Brewery.

One can but imagine how Thompson reacted when he first read Larkin's missive. But when he did reply, it was hard to believe this was the same man who had stood up from a meeting just weeks before. He wrote: 'Following careful thought and discussion in Dublin, your proposals were sent to the Parent Company for consideration prior to discussion with them. As you will of course know, several of the matters you raise are very much the concern of the Parent

Company, and not of the Dublin Company alone.' Thompson reported that he had met company chief Lord Boyd in London and it was agreed that they would discuss Larkin's proposals further under Parent Company chairmanship. Thompson advised that this could take several months and asked Larkin to let this be known to his union membership so they would not think that management was deliberately delaying. He concluded by asking that a proposed three-month trial of new work methods in the Spargers Section be supported by the union, as per discussions that had taken place with the men in the section. His tone was of a new man: 'I do ask that the Union assist in the implementation of this small re-organisation, for the trial period of three months, on the lines of the most recent proposals that have been put to them, and to which I honestly think they can take no reasonable exception.'

The workers in the Spargers Section accepted the three-month trial – and the upgrades that went with it. When informed, Thompson wrote to Larkin saying he was 'delighted that the Union has now been able to accept the Board's proposals'.

In the midst of all this brewery drama Jack Harte became yet again a hero when, in April 1962, he saved a boy's life. The boy had fallen into the water at North Wall and Jack, in working clothes and boots, jumped in to rescue him. The boy was panicking and almost brought Jack down with him, but Jack managed to bring him to safety. The story was in the newspapers and Jack was given a prize of ten pounds by the Brewery, presented to him by Lord Iveagh.

In three sessions on 3, 11 and 19 July 1962 Sir Geoffrey Thompson and his team sat down with Larkin, Carruthers and Harte to discuss Larkin's letter of 28 February. It was another revolutionary event in the history of the Company's industrial relations. Larkin, treated with suspicion when Guinness workers were opting for the WUI (which Harvey had in those early days described as the 'wrong' union to choose) had produced a document that had been studied and discussed at Board level in Dublin and London. Thompson wanted to outline the Board's detailed response.

Thompson's tone was in general one of acceptance. The Board wanted to find a way forward. Larkin, who wrote up an extensive report on the set of meetings, noted that the Board viewed the letter as containing two main elements: 'First, that all concerned in the work of the Brewery wished to know what is happening and to be afforded an opportunity of putting forward their views, and that all should share more directly in the fruits of any prosperity which may flow to the Brewery. The second point appeared to be that if there is co-operation in putting into effect new methods and introducing new machinery, the result must not be the loss of jobs, of gradings, either of the worker directly concerned, or of his colleagues anywhere in the employment.'

The word 'co-operation' was one that Thompson spoke much about: Guinness did not have a bottomless purse, and if the company were to remain competitive and profitable it had to have co-operation from its employees as it sought to improve efficiency in order to secure the future of the Brewery. Profits were a by-product of maintaining a healthy, efficient and competitive company – which in turn could offer more security to all its employees.

Thompson acknowledged that increased efficiency meant, in turn, labour saving. The company had a very low labour turnover – averaging only 2-3 percent per year among non-tradesmen – and an ageing workforce, so redundancy would be an issue. Company forecasts were that there would be a total of 290 redundancies over the coming five years (that would mean more than one in ten non-tradesmen). Management promised to pace the rate of modernisation so that the level of redundancies did not get out of control. It also promised to seek work elsewhere in the Company for any worker facing redundancy, and failing that to pay 'one week's wages for each year of service over 21 years of age, in addition to any deferred pension rights that might be earned.'

Thompson moved on to the other aspects of Larkin's letter. He said that the Company conceded to the Union's opinion that a 'prosperity bonus' should exist and would be an incentive for workers to have a more direct interest in the prosperity of the Company. The formula for that bonus had not been finalised, but the company wanted to keep it separate from a 'Christmas bonus' which had become seen as a gift from the company and that was how the Company wished to keep it. A further union proposal was the 'productivity bonus'. Here, he said it was difficult to find a good definition of 'productivity' – did it mean production of more barrels? Of more profit? How can an individual's contribution be quantified? The concept seemed to fall somewhere between the already established Christmas and prosperity bonuses. It was a subject that needed more study to find a solution.

Thompson then turned to the subject of consultation. Larkin wrote in his notes a comment that must have been music to his ears as Thompson spoke it: 'He agrees that what is needed is consultation and two-way communication throughout the Brewery, not just the establishment of a channel for the carrying of Management's decisions down to the men who must carry them out.' Sir Geoffrey had caught up with the changes in the Brewery he was running. Thompson did not, however, favour Larkin's proposal of a Joint Productivity Committee, feeling it would be unwieldy and ineffective. He suggested more communication within departments, with input from other departments if the need arose. His main concern was to keep the communication local for the sake of clarity and for ease of reaching decisions. He was willing, however, to try find a workable form of 'central machinery' for discussion on changes. To that end, he proposed an exploratory general meeting – of representatives not only of staff, management and so on but also from the Parent Company in London – to see what form such a committee might take.

It must surely have been electrifying to sit in that room and hear Sir Geoffrey Thompson deliver these decisions on behalf of the Board. In the course of those three sessions, a new union/management ethos was created. Whatever challenges lay ahead – and there were many – at least now there was no other view than that this would be a journey shared by equals.

As 1962 continued, the Workers' Union of Ireland Number 9 (Guinness) Branch went from strength to strength. By August 1962 final agreement was reached on the Five-Day Forty-Hour Week, to be launched Monday 5th November, by which time the Brewery had made final adjustments to work rosters to make it possible. It was one of the great visions of the trade union movement.

In September the WUI Foremen's (Guinness) Section was established. This was yet another trade union landmark. The rank of foreman had been the wall dividing non-tradesmen from management. There was already a house association of foremen, but in this new development the Foremen's Section issued a recruitment circular in which they wrote:

> House Associations have neither the strength nor the capability to uphold the dignity of workmen, whether they be foremen or not, as the history of such bodies in the Brewery bears testimony.
>
> Skilled negotiation ability is not acquired overnight, it requires a natural aptitude, combined with years of wide experience and specialised training, and in Mr Larkin, who will represent us, we have one of the foremost Trade Union leaders in this country.

When Larkin was approached by this new grouping, which was headed by Vincent O'Hara who had been a WUI shop steward before rising to foreman grade, he warned that he was limited in the extent to which he could represent them unless a majority of the foremen joined. To attempt to raise the membership numbers, a meeting of the Foremen's Association was held in the Rupert Guinness Hall on 25 September 1962. O'Hara, acting Chairman of the new Foremen's Section, was pitted against the Chairman of the Association.

O'Hara wrote a letter afterwards to Larkin informing him of how the meeting went. The Chairman pointed out that the thirty-three Tradesmen Foremen in the Association were already members of their own unions but this would not prevent the entire Association affiliating to the WUI if that was what the majority wanted. Vincent O'Hara, stated that 'he believed the high standard of wages and conditions which we enjoyed were due primarily to the role played by the WUI for the workers. He was convinced that had not the lower paid groups been raised so considerably, there would not have been any Grade 1, 1A, 1B or supervisors created.' But the Association Chairman dismissed this, pointing out that 'while the lower grades had their wages doubled in recent years, the foremen had theirs trebled'.

Mick Kiersey, long moved on from his years forming the Association of Brewery Employees and of bringing the WUI into the Brewery, expressed some frustration: 'Mister Kiersey said he was in the dark. Would someone, he asked, tell him whether the aim was to affiliate the Association to the WUI, similar to the Aer Lingus Pilots' Association, which he said would rule out the Trades Foremen, or was it the intention to form a new section affiliated to the Union, which would break up the Association as the Trades Foremen would also be on the outside.'

Concluding his letter to Larkin, O'Hara wrote:

> Open discussion followed during which it became very clear that Supervisors and Trades Foremen openly opposed any change of status or affiliation. However a ballot was held and Mr O'Hara was appointed one of the scrutinisers. The result was as follows:
> For: 26 Against affiliation: 107.
> This latter figure includes supervisors, 20, and Trades Foremen, 33.
> So it would appear that for the present, a minority will carry on the good work.

A week before Christmas, Jack Carruthers wrote to Sir Geoffrey Thompson: 'It is my pleasant duty to convey to you personally, and to your colleagues on the Board, the sincere good wishes for a Happy Christmas and Prosperous New Year from the members of the Branch Committee.' The Union and this new man they were dealing with on the Brewery management side had found each other's stride and could get on with the work they needed to do together for the benefit of both sides. But, as Harte said, this was a time when he and Jack Carruthers were facing 'oceans of work'.

Nine

Working Life

.

It's ironic that one of the leading figures in winning the forty-hour five-day week for the Guinness non-tradesmen rarely had a minute's respite from work day or night. Jack Carruthers had asked James Larkin for help to get a phone in his house in late 1955: since he represented men who were also shift workers, he felt it was important to always be contactable. He may have rued the day that the phone was installed.

Carruthers was in an unusual, and unenviable, situation: Branch Secretaries of the union usually worked from the WUI headquarters, but in the Guinness brewery Carruthers and Harte had, at the request of management, an on-site office. While this helped speed communication when there were issues to be dealt with in the ever-changing workplace, it also increased the workload on them. Carruthers had the additional complication of living in a house in one of the Guinness housing developments – Derravaragh Road in Terenure – so his neighbours were Guinness workers who sometimes came knocking at his door in the evening or at weekends for help with problems. Jack Carruthers turned no one away and so the demand on his time was relentless. When he did get home in the working week evening it was often just to grab a quick meal before heading off to some meeting.

Jack Harte recalled that meetings often went on so late that the men would miss the last bus and have to walk home. Worse still, meetings would run too late for the men to get to the pub for a pint before closing time! One union member used this to his advantage and would always seek some amendment when it was a quarter hour before pub closing time: his amendment was usually quickly passed so that the meeting could end and the men could get to the pub on time.

Harte recalled that some workers who came to the on-site office wanted the impossible, others wanted the illegal and others were lonely and wanted some company. Men would come for all kinds of reasons, including seeking family advice. One shop steward would come and sit with Harte and Carruthers to discuss issues and would always be very calm and pleasant while in the meantime constantly doodling on a sheet of paper. When he left, Harte would see that this man had been making a drawing of him and Carruthers with knives and dive bombers attacking them! Harte said: 'Jack and I never had a full dinner in the canteen. There'd always be somebody over our shoulder wanting help. We couldn't even walk out for a ramble: there'd be someone wanting to talk with you.'

Carruthers and Harte had a nickname for the workers who were most awkward or most difficult to deal with: 'the heavyweights'. Harte recalled: 'It wasn't just about dealing with management all the time. It was about dealing with the men on the factory floor. And there were some terrible awkward bastards. I took my coat off a couple of times: one time, fellas were on unofficial strike and they were laughing, saying to me 'it's just a long break we're having' and I blew my top and one of them was getting very aggressive so I said to him 'come on and we'll get this finished with' and fellas were pulling us back from each other. Thank God!'

Jack Carruthers had succeeded in bringing the Guinness workers on the boats into the WUI. The men were already members of the Seamen's Union, and so a lot of negotiation was involved between Jack and that union. His view was that the men were Guinness employees and would have more security – in the event, for instance, of redundancy – if they were under the protection of the WUI. Carruthers also unionised the Guinness provincial stores in Cork, Ballinasloe, Sligo, Galway and Limerick. This added travel to his workload, and he would sometimes delegate such trips to Harte. When union conferences were held outside Dublin, Harte and other men would share a car and stop off for a pint from time to time along the way. Carruthers, a life-long lover of motorbikes and never very at ease in a pub, would travel alone on his bike to save time.

In the Brewery, times kept on changing. The brutally tough job Jack Harte had held when he started work in the kieves, shovelling spent grain in steaming heat down to railway carts below, was now done with the press of a button. The Brewery already had the largest 'tun' (fermenting chamber) in the world and then built one more than twice that size: it could ferment almost two and a quarter million pints at one brewing. The brewhouse was being rebuilt and the Brewery was a mass of scaffolding and construction work. Jack Carruthers wrote a piece for the *Harp* magazine about the Lady Patricia, a highly modernised addition to the Guinness fleet. Everything was on the move.

Harte and Carruthers worked on the broader tasks of better pay and conditions for the workers in these changing times but also dealt with individual cases. Their workload meant that they could not always give quick attention to every problem. Once, Jack Harte came to Jack Carruthers angry that a man had come up to him, in front of everyone, and pressed a five pound note in his hand in the hope that Harte would expedite a matter he was dealing with on behalf of the man.

'I wouldn't take the money,' Harte told Carruthers, annoyed that the man would try to compromise him.

'You were right,' Carruthers quipped. 'You should have told him to put it in an envelope.'

On another occasion Jack Carruthers pursued a case for a Guinness driver who had been injured in a lorry crash. This man was given the huge compensation sum of ten thousand pounds – enough money to buy a house in those days. A week after he received the money this man ran after Jack to thank him and pressed a gift into his hand: an ounce of pipe tobacco.

Meetings to report to the trade union members were a regular part of the duo's work. Jack Harte recalled that these could sometimes be pretty hairy. The two men learned how to handle meetings: Harte said that they knew how to read the body language of men at meetings and could tell who might cause problems. They learned how to identify the most intelligent man at a meeting and focus on him. They also learned that the most important thing of all was to keep a cool head. As Harte said: 'If you blew your top at all, you lost the meeting.'

Being a trade union representative is a stressful life. Jack Carruthers gave himself completely to his work, but there were increasing strains in his home life. Jack Harte often noted that his colleague was preoccupied or tense. Sometimes, as they were on their way to a meeting, Carruthers would ask Harte to lead the meeting, saying he couldn't recall the details of the agenda. Once the meeting started Carruthers would soon take over and he knew every last detail. 'He knew it all backwards,' Harte recalled. 'He was a quick thinker at the table and had a gift for understanding legal issues. He was a brilliant man and a great team worker. I had great respect for him and the Union and its members benefited greatly from his work.'

Harte remembered one time a disgruntled shop steward dealing with a Job Evaluation issue came to Jack's office furious with him for writing a letter in which he had disclosed too much.

'That's your letter! That's your mistake!'

Jack took the letter and read it. He knew he was in trouble.

'That's your signature and that's your mistake,' the man yelled. 'You won't get away with this.'

'This is my letter?' Jack said.

'Yes.'

'Okay.'

Jack tore the letter up, then wrote a new letter correcting the mistake.

'Carruthers' quick thinking saved the day for both of us,' Harte recalled,

'However, down the line our representatives on the Job Evaluation Panel made life difficult for us when the ball was in their court.'

A huge frustration for Carruthers, in the light of all this strain and ceaseless work, was the apathy of the trade union members he represented. He often complained about that and was relentless in pursuing trade union members who did not pay their dues. He would write to Larkin with a list of offenders asking that they be threatened with expulsion from the Union – which in turn, given the agreement between the WUI and the Brewery, would mean the loss of their jobs. Carruthers also had to walk a tough line: he sometimes had to stand up to the men he represented as much as he stood up to management. He once ordered that a shop steward be removed from his union position for a year because the man had led an unofficial stoppage. He also had to remove a friend from the position as shop steward because he had not been handing over the Union dues to the office. Inevitably, being in such a position at such a crucial time meant that Carruthers picked up his share of enemies – including one worker who called him 'the Brewery Al Capone'. Carruthers ignored offers from management to switch sides and move over to the personnel department, which would have been much more lucrative for him. The principle of what he was doing, and his commitment to the labour movement, kept Carruthers going. The price was high.

Despite the constant industrial relations work, the nuts and bolts of union life needed attention. The Branch had set up a Financial Sub-Committee (which included Paddy Cardiff) to 'examine the Financial Organisation of No. 9 Branch and seek to eliminate any defects or flaws in the present system'. Their report came under three headings. The first area that needed better control, they felt, were those collecting union dues. There had been cases of abuse in this area and so a rigid set of rules was proposed: money collected must be paid in every three weeks and could not fall into arrears; arrangements had to be made for such things as the collector going on holidays or a union member temporarily transferring from one section to another; union collection cards should be available for inspection when requested. Under the heading of 'expenses' the sub-committee recommended a formalising of payments to members of the Branch Committee for costs they incurred in service to their union work. Under the heading of 'general situation' they recommended the purchase of such items as a desk, a telephone and a dictaphone. Not what you'd call an extravagant set-up!

Paddy Cardiff's great passion in his trade union work in the Brewery was education. He is quoted in Francis Devine's book about Cardiff's trade union career as saying: 'I was Chairman of the Education Committee in Guinness. Al Bates was Secretary and he got the 'Bulletin' (WUI magazine). I got a great deal from Jim Larkin that whatever Bulletins we sold, we could keep the money and use it in the education programme because there was no budget . . . Our programme was industrial relations primarily. The whole thing was to put forward the union's activities and all the business that was going on, which was substantial on a day-to-day basis . . . We always had Jim to speak on matters of collective bargaining and industrial relations, he was marvellous at all that.'

Cardiff felt that Bates' work on the education programme had much to do with the success of the Union in the Brewery.

Aside from friendship and the Union work, Carruthers and Harte also shared the same political views (Harte had been a member of the Labour Party since 1949) and even established a branch of the Labour Party – the re-formed Bluebell/Ballyfermot Branch. There were several brewery employees in the branch including Charlie Evenden, the former boxer who had been the first brewery policeman to join the WUI, who was on the committee. A man named George Butler was the secretary and wanted to get the nomination from the committee to go for election as a city councillor. Carruthers and Butler didn't get along and so Carruthers tried to find anyone else to go for the nomination – no one did. Butler was ultimately elected as a councillor. Harte and Carruthers canvassed for and helped Frank Cluskey, a man who later became head of the Labour Party. But the Branch they founded slowly wound down because the workload was too much and there were not enough people to share the weight.

Terrible personal tragedy struck in the midst of all this work and stress. Gerry Sharkey, a shop steward in the Brewery, and Jack Carruthers were very good friends and were neighbours on Derravaragh Road. They both also had young teenage daughters and these girls were friends since childhood. In January 1964, Gerry's daughter Maureen was hit by a bus on her way to school and was killed. Ten days later, on 30 January, Jack's daughter Anne collapsed suddenly at home and was rushed into hospital where she died of a brain haemorrhage. Jack Harte was with Jack Carruthers in the union office when the call came about Anne's being taken to hospital and the two men went there together. Harte tried to reassure Carruthers that all would be well, but he recalled that Jack Carruthers somehow sensed that what had happened to his daughter was fatal.

Jack Harte wrote poetry and he once wrote a poem about his friend and ally of so many years Jack Carruthers. The full text of the poem is lost, but Harte recalled it as being a poem about a man 'oblivious to the traffic flying by, his mind was so set in the problems he was trying to cope with . . . He didn't hear the sentence passed, but he was in his own jail.'

On 4 June 1965 a small pale-red booklet was issued in the Brewery: the Productivity Agreement between Guinness and the WUI. It was the culmination of discussion and negotiation sparked by Larkin's letter of 28 February 1962 to Thompson. The opening page of the booklet stated: 'It has been decided that in view of our present and future trends in the use of automation and techniques designed to improve the quality of our product, and to improve productivity throughout the Brewery, it is necessary to draw up a Productivity Agreement between Messrs Arthur Guinness Son and Co (Dublin) Ltd and the Workers' Union of Ireland on behalf of their No. 9 Branch.'

The agreement set out aims as had been presented by Thompson to Larkin, Carruthers and Harte in July 1962: the need for mutual trust, the need for the Union's workers to accept changing work means and methods. But negotiations in the years since the 1962 proposals had brought significant changes: protection from redundancy or wage loss caused by new technologies; extensive financial incentives for early retirement; and the establishment of the Joint Production and Advisory Committee. The latter was lean and clear; headed by the Personnel Manager with four representatives of management and four of the WUI. The transformation of the Brewery would be overseen by an equal partnership.

The agreement brought increases in wages and annual leave. It also launched a Profit Sharing Scheme that was revolutionary for its day. And then it knocked down the final barrier that Jack Carruthers had written about with venom in his family memoir:

> A further major achievement and the one that transformed the Brewery was in forcing the Board to recruit 'staff' from the once despised Labour ranks, as in its 200 year existence 'staff' had always been recruited from the universities or from the affluent sections of Irish and British society.

The agreement concluded with the statement: 'A substantial number of appointments have recently been made to staff posts from those employed in non-staff posts in the Company. It is the intention of the Board that this policy will be continued where possible.'

Following this – and, indeed, trying to follow in the footsteps of the WUI's success – the craftsmen in the Brewery all united under one umbrella 'Group of Unions' to further their own interests by negotiating as one voice. The concept of 'new' trade unionism as brought to Ireland by 'Big Jim' Larkin had overwhelmed the genteel old ways of Guilds and House Associations. The rates of pay through-out the Brewery returned to their pre-war level of being among the highest in the country. The ageing workforce helped in the process of reducing staff: over the 1960s the brewery shed a fifth of its employees.

Carruthers and Harte continued to fight the cases of various workers and departments – there had never been an agreement so set in ink that they could not find loopholes and challenges. The two were in regular dialogue with Personnel Manager Chamney seeking to review cases where they were aiming for better upgrades for various members. More often than not, they managed some improvement. The final grade lines were drawn by the Job Evaluation Panel in February 1966 and Carruthers issued them to union members. Payments were also agreed for all grades under an 'Increased Efficiency' agreement.

Looking for every way to strengthen the Union, the WUI extended its influence to the eminent construction firm McLaughlin and Harvey whose builders often worked in the Brewery: these men working on the site were obliged to join the WUI. This was a process of dotting the last 'i' and crossing the last 't': all the most profound changes had happened for the Brewery, its management and its workers over the previous twenty years.

By the start of 1967 the Guinness Group had invested about thirty million pounds in the Dublin brewery. By that year, also, their annual profit reached almost ten million. Sales of Guinness were on the rise again in Britain as were sales of Harp Lager. A new Guinness brewery in Nigeria and a growing world market added to profits, though also to investment demands.

The year, however, saw the death of two of the Guinness company's most significant figures: Sir Hugh Beaver and Rupert Guinness, the 2nd Earl of Iveagh. Beaver, after a very honourable military career in both world wars, had been in charge of Park Royal from 1946 and in the twenty years of his leadership he brought everything from work study to product diversification and the *Guinness Book of Records* into what had been a one-product company. Rupert Edward Cecil Lee Guinness died of a heart attack at the fine age of 93 at his home in Pyford, Surrey. He had been a man as passionate about farming as he was about the Guinness company. From his humble living conditions with his new bride to his political struggle for better housing along with his donations of millions to its cause, Rupert was a testament to the humanitarian tradition of the Guinness family.

But if the workload was extreme for Branch Secretaries, it was even tougher for the General Secretary. James Larkin worked ceaselessly. His secretary, Fionnuala

Claffey, recalled that he would set out from the office in the morning and go from one meeting to the next until returning late in the afternoon. He would then stand in her office and dictate a series of letters and memos resulting from these meetings. Trade unionism was his life's blood, but it also drained him as it did many people dedicated to the Labour movement. This light of the 'thinking, intelligent movement' was about to be extinguished.

At the end of 1968 Carruthers sent the new edition of the *Guinness Book of Records* to James Larkin. On 12 February 1969 Carruthers received a letter from Denis Larkin stating: 'Dear Jack, as no doubt your colleague Jack Harte has explained to you, Jim is quite seriously ill. He was, nevertheless, well enough to ask me to acknowledge with sincere thanks your thoughtfulness in forwarding the book and the kind wishes.'

At age sixty four, Young Jim Larkin was dying of lung cancer.

Ten

Flowing On

By 1969 the working class people of Dublin had come a long way from the misery 'Big Jim' Larkin had found them in when he arrived in 1908. By the time James Larkin Jr died, he had completed his father's heroic work and undone much of the damage his father had done to the Irish Labour movement. Young Larkin had been instrumental in reuniting the trade union congresses that had been split by one of the many battles between his father and William O'Brien. He had an even bigger aim: to reunite the trade unions that had been split when his father created the Workers' Union of Ireland when he lost control of the Irish Transport and General Workers' Union he had founded. It was an aim that yet again defined the way in which the son's vision towered over the father's ego. He believed in strength through unity, not in 'Larkinism' of any variety, and knew that a divided Labour movement would always be weak. The two unions came close to reunification in 1968, but negotiations failed.

Around the same time the general secretary of the ICTU, Ruaidhri Roberts, had called for an end to the multiplicity of unions representing workers (in Ireland at the time 86 unions represented 560,000 workers whereas in the Federal Republic of Germany 16 unions represented six million workers). Negotiations sought to bring the WUI's 30,000 members and the ITGWU's 150,000 members together. Sadly, that reunification did not happen in Young Larkin's lifetime. It would be some twenty more years before the WUI and the ITGWU joined to form SIPTU – the Services, Industrial, Professional and Technical Union.

'Big Jim' lived to the age of seventy-two, his son only to the age of sixty-four. The father died on 30 January 1947, the son on 18 February 1969. President de Valera attended the Requiem Mass at which the coffin was draped in the flag of the Workers' Union of Ireland and was flanked by a guard of honour of the WUI's officials. De Valera, as Taoiseach, had attended the funeral of 'Big Jim'. Many thousands lined the route as the cortege made its way to Dean's Grange cemetery: as with his father, on the day of Young Jim's funeral there was a snow blizzard. Older union men at the graveside commented on the similarity between the funerals of father and son.

Jack Harte wrote a moving tribute to Larkin for the *Harp* Magazine. In it he stated:

> The Larkin that I knew deliberately avoided overshadowing the memory of his father. Although an independent man, he was quick to abrogate that independence when the call to Labour sounded. His unwavering courage, his knowledge of himself and his occupation, his self-control and his keen sense of justice will live on with us to help us face the tasks ahead. Definite in his decision and plans and in applying them diligently, he was an inspiration to his followers.

Larkin's younger brother Denis took over as General Secretary of the WUI. Denis Larkin was not like his father or his brother. When he was James Larkin's deputy general secretary, his older brother often had to unravel chaos that he caused in his office. On one occasion, James was away for over a week and when he returned his secretary said she could not find important documents that where in Denis's office. James took off his coat, rolled up his sleeves and went in to his brother's office to sort everything in proper order. When Denis came back to his office the next day, he couldn't find anything!

Denis, like his father and his older brother, was a teetotaller. He was also very unpunctual. When he took over the running of the Union, his style was very different from that of his brother's. But while James had a very organised mind and

Denis did not, the younger brother had a great warmth and charm that his older brother lacked. Jack Harte recalled once going to the WUI head office in a rage over a letter Denis had failed to write for three months. When he arrived at the office, Denis greeted him with a big smile and, said disarmingly, 'come on and let's have a cup of tea' and handed him the letter.

Harte recalled Denis Larkin as a storehouse of knowledge and a great negotiator: 'he was a better hands-on man than Jim.'

Later in 1969, another of the key figures from the decades of change also exited the stage. In August, Jack Carruthers decided to quit his job as Branch Secretary and return to life as a Guinness worker. Not wishing to work for the management side in the Brewery he became a quality controller, travelling around the country to check that the Guinness being served was of the highest standard. Jack Harte reckoned that his friend was worn out after the long years of trying to balance the demands of trade union work and a difficult home life. In Carruthers' letter of resignation to Denis Larkin he wrote: 'I took over as Secretary in November 1953, thereby immediately sowing the seeds that finally broke up my marriage as having to attend meetings every evening, and Sunday mornings, left my wife feeling secondary to the cares of the men.'

Carruthers, looking back on the work he had done in the trade union in his family memoir, wrote: 'The real achievement was the establishing of the rights of the workers and a recognition of their inherent dignity as human beings.' He had played a huge role in that achievement. Jack Harte took over his friend's place as Branch Secretary.

When Jack retired, there was an outpouring of regret for his decision and admiration for his work. Jack Harte issued a statement 'to all members of No. 9 Branch, WUI' in which he wrote:

> You have learned of the resignation of our Branch Secretary, Jack Carruthers. For me personally, this is a very sad occasion, but it is an even sadder occasion for the branch members as a whole.
>
> Jack created a structure which was described by the late General Secretary as the best organised branch in the British Isles. Through

his organising ability every member had been given ready access to immediate representation.

Jack, despite his domestic pressures, never failed to meet the wishes of the members. To meet these desires it very often necessitated neglecting personal matters. The result was that circumstances have led to his resignation.

To realise the present wage structure and job conditions, it took very good negotiating ability, skill and judgement. Jack possessed and applied those qualities to the advantage of the members and to the benefit of the representatives who had the privilege of learning from him.

Jack's colleague Gerry Sharkey, who stepped in as 'Acting Secretary' of the Branch, wrote: 'In a brief letter, it is not possible to do justice to your wonderful contribution to the very effective organisational structure, wage rates and conditions. Through your unselfish endeavours and through the application of your skills and judgement, you have helped to realise for the members of No. 9 Branch a standard and quality of services which equates with the highest available. My personal feelings will be stated on another occasion, when the opportunity of a fuller expression of gratitude will present itself.'

Desmond Kelly, on behalf of the Guinness Shop's Stewards Trades Council, wrote to Jack of their regret on hearing the news: 'The council wish to express their thanks for all the help and advice you offered in the past. The council has instructed me to wish you every success and happiness for the future.'

Guinness's Labour and Industrial Relations Manager, G. N. Cairns, wrote: 'I, personally, will miss meeting you in the future – you were a very worthy protagonist. Number 9 Branch has come a very long way during your years as Secretary, and many of the advancements must be credited to your skill and judgment.'

Guinness Personnel Manager Cecil Chamney sent an immediate handwritten letter in which he stated: 'Your departure from that onerous post will be received with the greatest regret by all those on whose behalf you laboured so devotedly and unstintingly. I have always admired your strength of purpose and your intelligent appreciation of the art of 'the possible'. As you remember you helped me on many occasions to assess and measure the feelings of those remote from my office, but so well understood by you. This was for the common good and I offer you my sincere thanks for your service to all at St James's Gate.'

Sir Charles Harvey had remained in friendly contact with Jack Carruthers since retiring. In 1968 Carruthers had sent him an Easter greetings card to which Harvey had replied with a card ending, joking: 'With all fond wishes to the 'head pest'.' When Sir Charles was informed of Jack's resignation, he sent a handwritten letter from his home in Surrey: 'My dear Jack Carruthers. I was very sorry to hear from Mr. Hutton that you have given up the Secretaryship of No. 9 Branch and he sent me a copy of the very nice letter you wrote to him. You have been a very loyal and good friend of the brewery, and though at times we had our battles, you were always reasonable, and controlled your hot-heads. The brewery will miss you very much, and I only hope your successor will be equally reasonable.'

A few months later Sir Charles Harvey, having enjoyed eight years of retirement, died on 11 October at his home at Hampton Court Palace. A tribute to him in the *Harp* Magazine concluded: 'His tangible memorial is the Rupert Guinness Hall towards the building of which he gave every priority at his command. His intangible memorial is the memory we retain and the example he set. He was certainly not all things to all men. He was himself to all men, and all men respected him and loved him for this. We are all the richer for his having been among us.'

As this sad year came to a close an extraordinary era in the life of the Guinness brewery came to an end. Times change. People – and companies – move on. Jack Harte became a senator for the Labour Party in 1973. He went into the senate at the same time as Lord Iveagh – and one newspaper had a photograph of them entering the senate together with the caption 'The shop steward and his boss'. The two later became friends. Harte was re-elected senator seven times.

Change continued in the Brewery. In 1974 management introduced The Development Plan which formed the next wave of restructuring: three thousand permanent and casual jobs were to be cut over the following five years. Compulsory retirement at age fifty-five was introduced and so Harte retired from Guinness in 1975, after almost thirty years' service. 'When I retired, there was still a lot of discussion about lay-offs and productivity,' Harte recalled. His successor, Tom Garry, and Branch Chairman Willie Doyle had to take on that challenge. For all that the union had achieved over the decades, labour-saving became the main aim of the company and union/management discussions focused mainly on how to reduce staff numbers in an orderly and fair manner.

Jack Harte's wife Maud died of cancer on 16 December 1977. One of Jack's responses was to throw himself even more into work for the Labour movement. He did more in support of Labour leader Frank Cluskey, taking on constituency duties, but declined to seek election to the Dáil. After seven years of widowhood Jack met the woman who would become his second wife, Myra. Jack, aged ninety-one, is still going strong and was a huge help in the writing of this book. When he eventually started to renew contact with colleagues from the Guinness brewery Jack was happy to have so many workers greet him and thank him for the help he had given them in their struggles. He had witnessed a total transformation from a time when trade unionism was resisted in the brewery to a time when every member of staff at every level was a member of a branch of the Workers' Union of Ireland.

Jack Carruthers retired from Guinness's employ in 1981. By then, there were even more sweeping changes happening in the Brewery with the cutting of a further thousand jobs and heavy investment in new technology and work practices as St James's Gate evolved into one of the most modern breweries in the world and also took over United Distillers and became a multinational. It was another world, far from the days when Harvey, Carruthers and Harte worked in the Brewery.

In March 1989, Jack Carruthers died suddenly of a heart attack. Guinness colleague Willie Walsh wrote an obituary in the *Harp* magazine in which he stated:

Many of the agreements he negotiated throughout this period are still in operation today. His willingness to share his skills and to give encouragement, support and advice to young activists was largely responsible for the development of many of the future representatives within the branch.

On a personal basis, he held the respect of all who came in contact with him. He was at all times pleasant, courteous and was always willing to make allowances for the shortcomings of others.

We wish to acknowledge our debt of gratitude to Jack and we feel he would be happy in the knowledge that the work he did on behalf of the branch and the Union will live on in his memory.

In the year of Jack's death, there was a success story built on the shoulders of Carruthers and men like him that perfectly defined the breaking down of the Guinness hierarchy and levelling of the pyramid.

Finbarr Flood had joined the Brewery as a messenger boy in 1953 and recalled times when he was fined a shilling for looking at his boss the wrong way. He rose to become managing director of the Brewery in 1989, having been told when he first broke through into 'staff' as a clerk that he would not rise any further in the company. Without those dedicated to the growth of the Workers' Union of Ireland in the Brewery, who broke the hierarchy that had held the workers down, the success of this gifted man would never have been possible.

The influence was also felt on the side of the workers: three of the men who had worked with Harte and Carruthers in the Guinness union went on to senior trade union positions: two branch secretaries and one general secretary. Paddy Cardiff, Tom Garry, Joe McGrane, Eddie Higgins and John Graham are some of the people Harte listed as men who emerged from WUI No. 9 Branch to become full-time trade unionists. As Jack Harte recalled of his friend Jack Carruthers: 'Jack built up a great network of Chief Shop Stewards and Shop Stewards. When Jack was gone and I was gone, our successors had been drawn to the Union because of the influence of Jack. He was the one who created that network and it was one of his great achievements. It's to their credit that the shop stewards developed each of their sections so that they could deal with college-educated management.

We learned to recognise the intelligent men in the Union and focus on them.'

The intense days of the struggle for workers' rights have long gone. Guinness and the Irish Management Institute initiated the Charles Harvey Award for 'Outstanding Performance in a Business Masters Course'. 'Big Jim' Larkin's statue, his arms outstretched in an iconic pose, is on O'Connell Street in the company of other Irish legends such as O'Connell and Parnell. Guinness, through its expansion, evolved into being part of the multinational alcoholic beverages company Diageo. As Finbarr Flood states in his book: 'the majority of people in Guinness in Ireland with long service retired from the company; those who have come into the company since see themselves – quite correctly – as Diageo employees'.

There had been a time when Diageo management were considering closing down and selling off the St James's Street brewery but in the end, in 2004, it was Park Royal that was closed and sold off and brewery work consolidated in Dublin.

Nowadays, the Guinness Storehouse is the most popular tourist destination in Ireland – and it makes, indeed, for a very impressive experience. The perfect pint is still being brewed there, too, with scientific proof that the best Guinness pint is pulled in Ireland! But the process has been reduced to a fine art and brewery staff reduced now to less than one thousand: of whom most are contractors. One person at a computer now does the work of ten people manually in the past. The hardship is gone. Guinness remains a much-loved drink; three million pints of it are produced in the Brewery every day. But what goes around comes around.

In 1969 the Guinness Staff Association was formed. This evolved, in 1974, into an officially recognised trade union which was granted a 'negotiation license' in 1977. It became affiliated with the Irish Congress of Trade Unions in 1979: after all the struggle beginning in 1946 that led from the Association of Brewery Employees to the Workers' Union of Ireland, an Association finally became the voice of the workers: even if that workforce had been greatly reduced over the years.

There are no statues to the many great men who, awakened by 'Big Jim' and inspired by 'Young Jim', fought for and gained workers' rights in the Guinness brewery and throughout Dublin and beyond. Their memorial is their legacy. We now live in an age of equality that will hopefully continue to develop until all men and women, in all walks of life, are equal.